W9-ADF-352

Love-Based Money & Mindset:

MAKE THE MONEY YOU DESIRE WITHOUT $ELLING YOUR SOUL

by Michele PW (Michele Pariza Wacek)

Love-Based Money & Mindset: Make the Money You Desire Without Selling Your Soul.

This book may be purchased for educational, business, or sales promotional use. For information, please email info@michelepw.com.

ISBN 978-1-945363-01-6

Library of Congress Number: 2017902274

Contents

Introduction —
How It All Began

In 2014, I published my first Love-Based Copywriting book.

To be clear, copy (and/or copywriting) has nothing to do with protecting your intellectual property or putting a copyright on something. The term refers to written promotional materials for a business. And since businesses need a lot of things written (think website pages, email campaigns, social networking copy), copywriting is actually a pretty big industry that offers lots of opportunities, especially to freelancers.

What I ended up specializing in is something called "direct response" copywriting and marketing. In a nutshell, it's designed to get the reader to take action. Consequently, when you use direct response copy and marketing in your business, the copy does a lot of the heavy lifting for you by attracting leads/prospects, making sales, etc.

So, rather than having to go out and network, meet people one-on-one, follow up one-on-one, and then finally make the sale one-on-one (never mind actually delivering what you sold), direct response copy can do all of that for you, one-to-many.

In other words, direct response copy leverages your marketing activities.

You've probably seen this kind of copy in action. If you've ever received an email asking you to click on a link, or if you've ever found yourself reading one of those really long sales letters online where you're scrolling down looking for a price, all the while wondering to yourself "Do these things actually work?," you have read direct response copy.

(And the answer is yes. They do work!)

The problem is, traditional direct response copy and marketing can sound really hype-y, sales-y, and slimy. (Think used car salesman, droning late-night infomercial, etc.) And a lot of entrepreneurs (especially if you consider yourself conscious or heart-centered or mission-driven or spiritual or creative, etc.) really hate the idea of using anything that sounds arm-twisty in their business.

This is exactly why my entrepreneurial friends started encouraging me to create a different way of writing copy altogether: a way that didn't feel so hype-y or sales-y.

For years I resisted. I didn't really want to create an "other." The last thing I wanted was for people to say, "Well, if you're not serious about your business, you can go use this 'conscious' or 'attraction' copywriting. But if you're ready to pull up your big girl panties, then you should use traditional copywriting."

I wanted to transform the entire traditional direct response copy industry, NOT just offer an alternative.

I just wasn't sure how.

So, when my friend Susan Liddy brought "Love-Based Marketing" to the world, I was immediately drawn to it. After studying what she was doing, it struck me: "Love-Based Copy."

And that's when it all fell into place.

You see, in order to persuade anyone to do anything - it doesn't matter what it is; get the kids to go to bed on time, convince someone to go on a date with you, sell someone your product or service - you need to tap into that person's emotions. And all emotions basically fall under one of two categories: love-based or fear-based.

Love-based emotions include love, hope, joy, gratitude, peace, faith, trust, confidence, happiness, connection, forgiveness, openness, passion, freedom, harmony, honesty, compassion, self-love, self-appreciation, respect, acceptance, understanding, etc.

Fear-based emotions include fear, anger, grief, shame, guilt, bitterness, judgment, jealously, frustration, doubt, insecurity, etc.

Traditionally, most business models - and entrepreneurial mindsets - are based in fear. (And this isn't exclusive to business. Many things are built on a foundation of fear, such as government, organizations, advertising, etc.) The reason for this is that in many ways, fear is a dominant emotion (this includes any of the fear-based emotions such as anger, shame or grief/sadness).

Many, many folks live their lives being controlled in some way by their fear-based emotions. Either consciously - they're angry/depressed/grieving/judgmental/fearful/worried/unhappy/etc., or subconsciously - when they feel an uncomfortable emotion, they run away from it, bury it, hide from it, etc. (Think about all the things that happen when someone gets upset: he starts a fight, takes a drink, overeats, goes shopping, gossips, etc.)

But if fear-based emotions are controlling your behavior, it's going to be very difficult to build anything love-based.

Now, just to be clear, being love-based doesn't mean you don't feel fear-based emotions. On the contrary, people who have embraced love-based businesses and lives in fact DO fully feel all emotions, both love-based and fear-based. There is definitely a place for fear-based emotions in our human existence, so rather than fight the fear-based emotions, the key is to feel them and let them move through you, instead of avoiding them. (Feelings just want to be felt, after all.)

Plus, because folks who have embraced the love-based mindset do feel fear-based emotions, it also means they aren't controlled by them. It's when you try not to feel the fear-based emotions that they really control you. If you don't feel your emotions, you stuff them away, and you won't fully release them until you feel them.

So, to bring this back to how this relates to copy, traditional direct response copy taps into fear-based emotions, which is why it feels so icky.

But you don't have to trigger fear-based emotions to sell. It is entirely possible to tap into love-based emotions, and sell with LOVE.

That understanding inspired me to write five books in my love-based business series:

- 💜 *Love-Based Copywriting Method: The Philosophy Behind Writing Copy That Attracts, Inspires and Invites .*

- 💜 *Love-Based Copywriting System: A Step-by-Step Process for Writing Copy That Attracts, Inspires and Invites*

- 💜 *Love-Based Online Marketing: Campaigns to Grow a Business You Love AND That Loves You Back*

- 💜 *How to Start a Business You Love AND That Loves You Back*

And of course, the one you're reading right now.

And the response has been amazing! Entrepreneurs love the love-based copy and online marketing philosophy, telling me it's exactly what they've been searching for.

However, the deeper I went into this work, the more I realized I didn't go nearly deep enough in my other books into one of the key foundational pieces, which is …

Mindset.

You see, if your mindset is not one of love and abundance, it's going to be very difficult (if not impossible) to write copy and market yourself in a love-based way.

For instance, let's say you've been in a financial dry spell for a while, and you're getting worried. You've got bills piling up, and you're not sure where the money is going to come from to cover them.

If you're in that headspace, and you sit down to write emails or you get on the phone with a prospect, it's going to be very difficult to not slip into the habit of using fear-based selling tactics. Maybe you suddenly find yourself mentioning how their worst fear might come true if they don't sign up with you, or using shaming tactics by saying something like, "Clearly, you aren't serious about X, or you would be throwing your credit card at me right now," just to make the sale.

Now if this has happened before, it's totally understandable. You need the money. You don't know when (or even IF) another prospect is going to knock on your virtual door. You feel like you've got to do something (anything!) to generate some cash.

And it's really, really scary to be in that situation.

So, of course you're going to do everything possible to make the sale. After all, you know in your heart that what you're offering is really good. It will help the person who buys it - so giving him or her a little push won't hurt. (Right?)

THEN, once you have money coming in the door and the bills paid, you can really focus on marketing the love-based way.

I get it. But …

It doesn't exactly work that way.

There are a lot of reasons why, which I cover later in this book, but in many cases, this leads straight to disaster. Bouncing between love-based and fear-based marketing depending on your bank account only creates confusion. Even worse, if you keep bouncing around between love and fear, chances are you're going to end up in the middle of a dark time when all of the sudden, nothing works, neither fear nor love, and your business starts to really tank.

If you want to market and sell yourself with love, then it's important to always use love-based copy and marketing, no matter what your financial situation looks like.

I also know that can be really difficult. And scary.

That's why I wrote this book.

I want to give you the tools to shift your mindset so no matter what is going on in your life, you're able to center and ground yourself in love and abundance (which will help you attract more of it into your life).

I also want to give you the tools to attract money, because it's a lot easier to have a mindset of love and abundance when you actually HAVE money and abundance.

But first ...

Who Is This For?

If you're a business owner/entrepreneur, this book is for you.

If you're a healer, coach, service provider ... keep reading.

If you dream of one day starting your own business, this is for you, too.

If you're not any of the above, no problem!

These mindset and money-attraction tools can help anyone attract more money into his or her life.

While many of the examples and stories I include throughout the book have an "entrepreneurial slant," the message and meaning behind those stories are still applicable to you.

How to Use This Book

I want to say right now that I am not an expert in mindset and money attraction. (I'm the copywriter/marketer, remember?)

That's why I interviewed my friends and fellow entrepreneur experts about their very best mindset and money-attraction tips and strategies, and I've based much of this book on their wisdom.

In fact, when I was right in the middle of my interviews, I realized I was writing the book I wanted to when I started my personal development journey in 2005. At that point, I looked for a book or resource that would give me a smorgasbord of all the different mindset and money-attraction strategies out there, so I could make a better, more informed decision about which were the right ones for me.

With that in mind, I've included a wide range of strategies and exercises around mindset and money attraction - everything from the super woo-woo to the very practical and down-to-earth. Everyone is different, and different strategies are going to work for different people, so if one of the exercises doesn't work for you, try something else! I'm confident you'll find something that resonates.

Also, some of what you discover while reading this book and completing the exercises may feel really uncomfortable, or even trigger you in ways you don't quite understand. You may find that you're drawn to some, neutral to some, and absolutely repelled by others. All totally normal!

I would love to invite you to stay open, even (and especially) in regard to the exercises and strategies that feel scary and completely out of your comfort zone.

I encourage you to give all of them a try, but you may want to focus on the ones you're drawn to AND the ones that repel you. Both of those reactions can be a sign that those particular exercises are exactly the ones that will help you make a big shift.

In addition, you're going to see about a million questions in here to ask yourself (for a time, I was considering calling this The Question Book).

Why? Because you need to actually ask the right questions to get the answers you're looking for.

If you're not getting the results you want, then you're probably asking questions that may not be "right" or appropriate for you. They may work for other people, and maybe they even worked for you at a different time in your life, but they're not in alignment with you now. In this book, you'll discover how to discern which questions are more appropriate for you now. In addition, I'm going to share more about how the brain works (and how your brain may actually be keeping you from the abundance you desire), but for now, here's the short version:

Your mind is similar to a computer: ask it a question and it will look for the answer. Once that answer pops up, you take action.

You start to create solutions, and then, you look for evidence that supports/proves that answer.

But if the answer isn't an answer that's actually moving you forward, you're going to be collecting evidence and taking action on solutions that aren't really going to give you what you want.

That's why this book provides you with new questions and new ways to ask questions - so you CAN start getting the results you want.

Sure, new ways of doing things can feel uncomfortable. But it's also SO exciting, because any time you encounter a new idea, it holds the possibility of completely shifting your mindset and your reality. (And that's what we're looking for here, right? A shift, so you can more easily attract money.)

All that said, I've divided this book into four parts.

Part One: We begin by talking about how to effectively deal with fear and fear-based emotions. This is key; it's MUCH easier to shift out of a fear-based mindset if you understand exactly what you're dealing with. I also share foundational pieces that will make it easier to start shifting your mindset into love and abundance.

Part Two: This is where you learn how to shift your mindset into one of abundance and love. (Yes, both are equally important if you want to experience more abundance in your life.)

Part Three: It's all about the money, baby! Now, if you're feeling stressed financially, you might be tempted right now to skip directly to this part. I would encourage you to quash that desire. It's not that these money-attraction strategies won't work if you do - they will. However, not only will they likely be easier to implement if you've first done the work around love and abundance, but the shifts will be more likely to "stick." Plus, as you'll see later, I suspect you'll be a lot happier - and more at peace overall - if you do the work in order.

Part Four: Here, we focus on how you can take everything you learned and apply it to your business.

Remember, each section contains specific tips and exercises to help you start implementing the teachings as quickly as possible, so you can start seeing the results you want most, so be sure to complete them as you go.

Finally, I want to take a few moments to talk about the word "God." I know for some of you, the word "God" is a trigger, which is why I try and use other words as well, such as Universe, Source, Higher Power, etc. If you don't care for the word "God," just swap it out for whatever word you're more comfortable with - what works for you is absolutely what you should use.

Bonus Resources:

All of the expert interviews I hosted can be found in my Love-Based Money and Mindset Podcast Series, which I encourage you to listen to (especially those experts you are most drawn to in this book). You can do so at http://www.LoveBasedBizBlog.com

In addition, most of the experts I interviewed are offering a free gift to enhance what you learn in this book. Read more about these gifts in the Resource section at the end, and if you feel called to deepen your learning with any of them, their contact information and links can be found there as well.

Lastly, to help you shift your mindset and start attracting more money quickly, I've created a Money and Mindset Blueprint to go along with this book. It's designed to help you create a personal plan for shifting your mindset based on all the exercises. You can download it for free right here:

http://www.LoveBasedMoney.com/blueprint

Part 1

SETTING UP THE FOUNDATION

Chapter 1
WHERE IT ALL BEGAN

My journey as an entrepreneur started in 1998 when I quit my job to become a freelance copywriter.

And besides the super-nasty feast/famine model I created for myself, I did okay. I basically made around $50K for the first five years.

Except I didn't want to be making only $50K; I felt like I was working all the time for that amount of money. During the feast part of the cycle, I would work 60-70 hours a week, and during the famine part, I spent at least that much time per week worrying about my business.

In December 2003, I came to the horrible realization that I was STUCK at that income level. It didn't seem to matter what I did or didn't do - raise my rates, change my marketing - 50K was my ceiling.

And I knew there were freelance copywriters out there making six figures - so why wasn't I?

Well, at first I told myself it was because I lived in Prescott, AZ: a small town with a population of about 40,000. So, in 2004, I started branching out, using the Internet to increase my reach – to get more (and better) clients.

And I did get better clients. But I got fewer of them. And I still made only $50K that year.

About that time, I happened to see the Seinfeld episode where George decides to do everything opposite. At the beginning of the show, he had no girlfriend, no job, and no place of his own, living with his parents. At the end of the show, after doing the opposite of everything he normally did, he had a girlfriend and a job with the New York Yankees (although he hadn't managed to move out of his parents place yet).

So I thought, maybe I too needed to "do the opposite" in 2005.

One of the things I did was hire a coach so I could start working on myself. I figured I had tried all of these external, outer strategies (raising my rates, changing my marketing strategy, etc.) and they didn't work, so therefore I must be the problem.

And at first it appeared I was on to something! In 2005, I made over $70K and in 2006, I finally broke six figures.

Yay me, right?

Well ...

Even though I continued to grow my business and my income over the years, I never felt comfortable, or like I had finally "made it."

Before, when I was making $50K, I was sure that as soon as I hit that magical six-figure mark, all would be well. I would finally feel peace around my finances, instead of all that anxiety and worry.

Then, when I first hit the $100K mark and didn't feel any better (in addition to realizing that, with the added expenses, I didn't actually take home any more than I did when I was making $50K), I thought, "Well, I bet I'll stop worrying about money when I make $250K."

I hit that mark, and if anything, I felt more stressed and worried about money than I had before.

So, of course, I immediately figured I needed to make more money - because clearly I hadn't hit the "magic" number yet.

But it didn't matter how much money I made: my stress, anxiety and worry about money just continued to climb.

Until finally, in November of 2012, I just mentally collapsed. I started crying and couldn't stop. I had nightmares for two weeks. I was barely functioning.

Now, to be fair, it wasn't only the money that drove me to the collapse. I had been in a caretaking situation for some family members that year (including my mom, who had been diagnosed with cancer). Being a caretaker is … well, let's just say I'm not exactly caretaker material and leave it at that. So, all of that

17

additional emotional burden just piled on top of the anxiety I already felt around finances, causing everything to finally collapse.

What finally started to turn everything around for me was when, during that lost, crazy, state I was in following the collapse, a little voice cut though the darkness. It said: "Ten percent of life is what happens to you. 90% is how you deal with it. And how you're dealing with it right now is crap."

I immediately called a friend of mine, Christine Arylo, Spiritual Catalyst, Feminine Leadership Advisor, and Best Selling Author, and she became my spiritual mentor.

With her help, I not only recovered, but I thrived. My anxiety and worry are basically gone. I experience peace now (and joy and all sort of emotions I'm no longer too numb to feel … because I no longer stuff everything down).

And, the best part is that now, my emotional state is not tied to my bank account!

And, the best, best part is that because my emotional state isn't tied to my bank account any longer, I've been able to make even more money than I did before.

Now, if you're wondering exactly what I did to turn it all around, I promise I'll share it all, because if I can save you from the painful 2x4 that slammed me to the ground in 2012, that would be fabulous.

Plus, I want you to know that if you struggle with money, I get it. This is my struggle too. You are absolutely not alone.

Along with sharing my wins and my losses (including the times I totally fell on my face), I'm going to share other people's stories. Like I said in the Introduction, we're all different, and different things are going to resonate with each of us. My job is to cast the widest net possible, so to speak, so you get to experience that "ah-ha" moment around your money and mindset, and start shifting it.

So, I want to start with why, despite what you might have heard, all exercises and modalities don't work the same for all people.

Chapter 2
WHY DOESN'T IT WORK FOR ME?

In 2005, when I got serious about my personal development work, I met countless folks: some who became clients, and some who I simply chatted with at events. Over and over again, I'd hear the same thing: "I know the secret. I know why you didn't get results with X."

This was inevitably followed by some variation of the following: "MY system for getting rid of blocks/shifting mindsets/attracting money works better than all the other ones out there." Or, "The reason you didn't get the results you wanted from those other systems is because they were missing this key ingredient - which is in MY system."

At the time, I wasn't sure what to make of it. All these money and mindset experts had wildly different ideas as to what worked and what didn't. And it was especially confusing when I would try someone's system or exercise, and it wouldn't really work for me.

What was going on? Were they mistaken? Were they fooling themselves, having convinced themselves something worked when it really didn't? Or, worse yet, were they actually out-and-out lying?

I couldn't believe they were being deliberately misleading and making money off of something they knew didn't work, but none of those explanations were terribly reassuring.

It wasn't until I met Jeffrey Van Dyk, Creator of the Tribal Marketing Training, that I finally found an answer as to why there were so many different healing modalities out there, and why none of them work (or work the same) for everyone.

Jeffrey's work is around something called our "core wound."

Everyone has a core wound, and it was inflicted on each of us when we were children. Basically, something happened to us to make us feel unloved, and we created a story around it.

Now, a core wound doesn't result from a single incident. We have multiple wounding experiences, but typically find that we use the same stories to explain them all.

Brene Brown, best-selling author of *Rising Strong* (and other books), talks about how as humans, we have a propensity to make up stories to explain why bad things happen to us. It's in our nature to want things to make sense. So, we make up stories to MAKE it make sense. And, in the case of our core wounding, the stories we make up place the blame on ourselves.[1]

You see, we can't blame the person who actually hurt us - even if that person is hitting us or abusing us. As children, we depend on that person to house and feed us, so that person can't be to blame. Our survival is at stake.

So, it must be us.

---

1   Brene Brown, *Rising Strong* (2015)

Now, no matter what story we make up, a part of us, deep inside at our soul level, knows it isn't true. And that creates a separation inside - between the part of us that believes the wound-based story, and the part that doesn't.

That, my friends, is the core wound.

So, an example of a core wound is if your father told you over and over again that you are stupid. You may decide that he must be right, and you really are stupid. This core wound would then be the impetus for your spending your adult life getting various degrees or certifications - proving in external ways that you aren't stupid, although inside you're never able to rid yourself of that feeling that you are.

But, if we look deeper, past that wound, we know the truth - you are not stupid.

Other common core wounds include, "I don't belong," "I'm not enough," "I don't matter," "I'm bad," "I'm unwanted," "I'm unlovable," "I'm not worth it," and more.

I know this idea of core wounds may be a bit confusing, so I'm sharing a story from Pamelah Landers, Expert Relationship Wisdom for Your Work and Personal Life and Master Hand Analyst, (who you'll hear more from later in this book) now, to illustrate how your core wounds can affect your life and business.

Pamelah explained how it wasn't an easy process for her, to discover her core wound. In fact, she shed tears as she shared her stories with Jeffrey. Jeffrey told her, "Your wound is around not being seen." As the tears continued to stream down her face, she felt the truth in that statement, and it was so familiar to her, she couldn't deny it at all.

It's important to understand that one of the foundations of Jeffrey's work is recognizing the gifts that have come from your core wound. In other words, each of us has developed a very unique expertise that no other person has, based on our unique core wound. And the people who want to be with us are seeking those gifts.Pamelah was the second of six children, and her parents were perpetually busy with her younger siblings. They didn't have much time to focus on her, which she translated into being somewhat invisible. Having done "parts work" as an adult, where she was able to feel her six-month old self, she knew that even crying if she needed something would cause a disruption in the family. Consequently, being quiet - not heard or seen - meant she would feel safer. So she learned not to ask for what she wanted unless it was really necessary.

Not seen, not heard. In addition, Pamelah was molested at a young age, furthering the cycle of wanting to be invisible, so the molester wouldn't "see her." It served her to be hidden, and she was well-trained in the art of staying that way. To Pamelah, it wasn't really a choice; she felt like her survival and safety were at stake.

In her child's survival mind, all of this was interpreted as being "unseeable." And that was required in order for her to simply cope with her life.

However, even though she felt invisible a lot, fundamentally it wasn't TRUE. It took some unraveling of the core wound to separate her survival skills from who she actually IS, and to step into the world of visibility.

As Pamelah continued working with Jeffrey, she "looked for evidence of the wound being true." She also started looking for evidence of how she actually was seen, and she found it in unsolicited testimonials from clients and friends who called her because they knew she was the one who had insights for them. They saw her wisdom and insights ... they saw her brilliance.

Regular conversations with Jeffrey helped her to begin to notice the value of embracing her core wound, as she also realized that the wound "wanted to be done" – what Jeffrey calls "reaching the expiration date." Soon, Pamelah also came to understand that her tribe would have a similar core wound as hers. She started investigating further, asking deeper questions about how her core wound served her, emotionally and mentally. That began her journey toward embracing her wound, and toward acceptance, as she even learned how to laugh at herself at times realizing how much being seen actually mattered ... and how much emphasis she had put on staying hidden. One of the most healing "awarenesses" she discovered was that no matter how much other people acknowledged or "saw" her, it would never be "enough" until she truly embraced the value of the wound and could see herself. Before that happened, she couldn't really receive or take in what others told her. But when she finally could, that's when things shifted for her, and the core wound no longer unconsciously controlled her life. That's when she felt the freedom to share with her tribe the value of seeing themselves, giving them permission to embrace their dark side.And THAT'S when the truth of being seen, starting with herself, became a gift instead of a wound for Pamelah. She says that excavating the core wound has been life changing for her. She has grown personally and professionally as she incorporated her learning about her wound into her teachings. It's important to note that core wounds don't have to come from abuse. They can come from anything we misinterpret as children as a sign we aren't loved. Maybe our mother decided to go back to work while we were still young so we were raised by a nanny, and we took that to mean we are unlovable. (Because if we were lovable, our mother wouldn't have gone back to work and left us with a nanny.) Or maybe we had a perception that our parents always took our sibling's side in key arguments, so we felt like we were never heard, or we weren't important. Or, like Pamelah, maybe we were one of many children and it felt safer to not be seen (even without the sexual abuse, Pamelah still would have had that same core wound).

But, above all, remember that what is key about our core wound is that, on a deep, soul level, we know it isn't true. And, even if we're not fully conscious of that separation, we still feel it, and we act in a way that continues to prove it IS true, because it feels so foundational. This is exactly why some of us are drawn to healing modalities - so we can heal that separateness we feel within us.

The problem is, people create healing modalities based on the healing he or she went through around his or her particular core wound.

Which means, if your core wound doesn't match the wound of whoever created the modality, you may not get a lot out of it. (This is the basis of George E. P. Box's premise, "All models are wrong but some are useful.")

So, to give you an example, let's say your core wound is "I don't belong." If you do some healing work with someone who has that same core wound, it's likely you will experience a profound shift. But, if you do the work with someone whose core wound is "I'm bad," it may be interesting and somewhat helpful to you, but it's less likely to create a big shift.

When Jeffrey explained this to me, it was as if all the pieces finally fell into place. It suddenly made sense why some people would swear a certain system would fix everything, but when I tried it, it did little to nothing for me.

And that's why I've designed this book as a sort of sampler platter - so you can get a taste of many different healing modalities, upping your chances of finding one that works for you.

So, how do you discover your core wound? Hint: It's NOT about ignoring it, pushing it away, and/or doing whatever you can to keep it from coming into consciousness because it feels painful. The key - the ultimate work - is to embrace it.

EXERCISE: Discover Your Core Wound

A good way to start the process of discovering your core wound is to do some journaling. (In fact, you'll likely want to have a journal on hand as you read through this book.)

Begin by identifying five to six episodes from your childhood that really stand out to you because of the emotional intensity behind them.

Once you identify those experiences, do some deep journaling around each of them to really get at the emotions and stories behind them. Describe them in detail, using imagery. What did the experience sound like? Feel like? Look like?

After you finish journaling, go back and read what you wrote, taking a close look at the themes of each episode. Chances are you'll discover a common theme or story running through all of them.

When you do, you've found your core wound.

(And have some tissues handy, because if you're anything like me, once you discover it and actually identify with it, you'll start crying.

That's okay! And completely normal. There's a reason it's called a "wound" ... so let yourself cry, if you feel it.)

This work isn't easy, and some people find it incredibly difficult to do on their own. If that's you, and you'd like to find out more about Jeffrey, don't forget to check out the Resource section at the end of the book. (I also include more from him in Part Four, when I cover how your core wound can help you market and promote your business more effectively.)

Okay, so now that you've identified your core wound, you're probably wondering what to do about it.

There are three things to do, actually.

First, I'd like to invite you to shift your perspective on your core wound.

Instead of viewing it as a burden - some icky thing you're stuck dealing with throughout your life - try looking at it in a way that will allow you to reclaim the VALUE of it, instead. (And yes, there is HUGE value in your core wound.)

Think of your core wound not as something that happened TO you, but FOR you.

If you allow it, your core wound can actually be your greatest teacher and biggest ally. Along with helping you along your self-development journey, it can also help you market your business with more ease and less stress (more on that in Part Four).

Second, your core wound has layers - which means discovering and acknowledging it is simply the first step.

As each layer is integrated (and by "integrated," I mean you've accepted each layer as part of your BEING, as opposed to pushing them away or denying them altogether), a deeper layer is revealed. That's an invitation to go deeper and integrate even more of your core wound.

This is why, as you embark upon this journey, you may think you've dealt with an issue, and therefore, you assume it's done – you've conquered it. But then, you notice that it circles back on you (and typically when that happens, it's an invitation to integrate it at an even deeper level).

Again, totally normal. This is just part of the journey of life.

You may be thinking, "Well that sucks! Why can't I just deal with the wound and have it be done? I don't want to keep healing myself. I'll never get anything else done."

Pamela Bruner, Business Coach, Author, and EFT Tapping Expert says if you think that, it's because you have the wrong definition of what it means to "fix" or "get over" an issue. (I'll be sharing more from Pamela later in the book, as well.)

The thing is, if we stop growing - if we hit whatever goal we've set and don't set any new ones - then, yes, we won't need any more self-development work. But, chances are, once we reach one goal, we'll immediately set another, which means new blocks and issues will continuously pop up.

So, for instance, let's say we have an income goal of breaking six figures. And we reach it; we make $110,000. If we're done - meaning we don't raise the goal to break $250,000 - then we don't need any more self-development work. But, once we raise that goal, we're most likely going to need to go through a new set of issues or fears or blocks that are going to arise in reaction to that new income goal. This means you'll need to keep healing yourself.

Which leads me to a very important point: I don't really like to think of all of this work as "healing yourself."

You're not broken. You don't need to be healed.

In his book, *EMERGENCE: Seven Steps for Radical Life Change*, author Derek Rydall talks about the Law of Emergence. The bottom line is basically that you are already whole and perfect. It's your job to let your real, whole, perfect self emerge. Just like an acorn has a perfect little tree inside it that just needs the right soil and temperature and water to grow into a tree, our job is to cultivate an environment where we allow our whole, perfect self to emerge.[2]

2   Derek Rydall, *EMERGENCE: Seven Steps for Radical Life Change* (2015)

30

That's why this work is not about healing. It's about integrating emotions into your life/existence, instead of avoiding them. It's about integrating the uncomfortable feelings and emotions you've been pushing away or numbing or running away from … integrating the shadow parts of yourself you're ashamed of … and integrating the lessons of your core wound. And when you integrate them, you accept them as being just as important and legitimate to your existence as other "happier" emotions. (If you've never experienced this before, this probably sounds very strange to you, but I can guarantee if you do this, what's on the other side is a deep sense of peace and calm.)

A key part of integration is feeling emotions you don't want to feel, and loving and accepting parts of yourself you don't feel are worthy of love or acceptance. I'll talk more about this in the next chapter, and I'll provide you with some different ways to begin doing it.

Also, I want to add that yes, the first time you really dig in and try some of these processes, they may rock your world (and not necessarily in a good way). You also may very well discover you don't get a lot done, because processing your feelings takes over everything.

As someone who has been there, I can tell you that sometimes when you're processing something really big, you end up having a crappy day.

But, don't you have crappy days now?

At least for me, the crappy moments and days I experienced to get where I am now were ALL worth it. It was all worth the peace I now feel. It was worth breaking free from the constant worry and anxiety that controlled me, and definitely worth the feeling of freedom I now have because my emotions are no longer controlling me.

It was so worth the joy I have now.

Here's the thing:

You can't just numb the uncomfortable emotions without also numbing the good. So, if you're busy doing things to avoid feeling the uncomfortable stuff, you're actually not allowing yourself to feel the "good" emotions, either.

Another thing to keep in mind is when you do integrate the uncomfortable feelings, what ends up happening is that you also become able to release a lot of other undesirable stuff, like triggers (for example, you might find that you remain calm in situations because you DON'T react to things the way you used to).

You can release influences on yourself and your thinking you didn't even know you had (for instance, I used to be very concerned about what other people thought of me - now, not so much!).

And as an added "bonus," you'll also be able to finally hear your own inner wisdom/ guidance (which probably means you'll be following what you need to do for yourself, instead of acting on the influence of other people or external factors).

Even more importantly, the more you release the hold your uncomfortable emotions have on you, the easier it will be to actually do (and get results from) the exercises in this book. (I know that might not make a lot of sense right now. Just trust me on this, and keep going.)

In the next chapter, I'll go into more detail about fear-based emotions, and offer some modalities you can use to break the cycle of fear.

Chapter 3
BREAKING THE CYCLE OF FEAR

For almost my entire life, I was a massive worrywart.

I worried almost constantly about, well, everything.

I had an incessant, yammering voice in my head pontificating about pretty much anything and everything that could go wrong. Coupled with either the low-grade feeling of anxiety I nearly always felt - or the amped up, full-power anxiety I felt when things actually were heading south in a big way - what was going on in my head was a hot mess.

For years, I did my best to control and subdue that voice, but to no avail. When I finally cracked in 2012 from all those years of worrying and anxiety and beating myself up and everything else going on, in a way, it was almost a relief.

One of my coaches once asked me what the payoff was for my worrying. I couldn't think of a thing. I *hated* the sick feeling I got when I worried. Why on earth would I choose to feel that way?

Well, now that I've "broken the back" of my worrying habit, I've been able to look back and see that yes, indeed, my worry and anxiety definitely did have a payoff.

It was self-soothing. (Crazy, I know.) It also covered up other emotions I didn't want to feel, like anger and grief. Apparently,

I would rather feel anxiety than pretty much any other emotion, especially anger or grief.

I also used to use my worrying as a talisman. Since so few things I worried about actually came true, I almost felt like I HAD to worry about the bad things in order to keep them from happening. (As a side note, this part of my worrying habit was also the most difficult part for me to break.)

This "worrying as a talisman" thing led to a another interesting observation as well: when something bad happened out of the blue, I would actually feel guilty if I hadn't worried about it, because I thought if I had, it may not have happened at all. How's THAT for backwards?

I bring this up because if there's one emotion I have a great deal of knowledge about, it's fear. And, I can tell you with 100% certainty that my worry, anxiety and fear absolutely got in the way of my attracting more money.

No matter where you are right now, no matter how broke or stuck you are, working on your mindset around money is key to turning your money situation around. (Yes, even if you're feeling like you have "real" money problems and all this mindset stuff is well and good for people who aren't struggling as much as you are. I'm talking to you!)

This is the same thinking that caused the mess and noise in my head to get louder and more chaotic.

Plus, the more money I made, the messier my head became.

And, the more frantic the noise in my head got, the more frantic my external actions became ... and the less I was able to hear either the voice of my inner wisdom/intuition, or the voice of Source/The Divine/God.

So, when I was feeling stressed about money, it would typically look something like this:

- 💜 Worry: It felt so frantic. The thoughts were constantly spinning. What could I do to make more money? Are there any prospects I could call? Should I run a sale? Something else?

- 💜 Activity: This would be followed by a flurry of action on my part. Whatever I could do to solve the problem, I'd do it (which, in retrospect, was mostly pretty useless).

- 💜 Searching: Because I couldn't hear either Source/God or my own inner wisdom, I was constantly looking outside of myself for answers - asking other experts, buying products and programs, etc. Which, in and of itself wasn't the problem; I wouldn't be where I am today if I hadn't invested in myself and my education as an entrepreneur. But I was over-relying on other people's expertise and advice, instead of valuing my own. In turn, I made a lot of mistakes and wasted a lot of money doing things that were not necessarily a good match for me and my business. (As my good friend Andrea J. Lee says, "You spend all this time getting your ducks in a row, only to find out they're not your ducks.")

💜 Exhaustion: This was a given. At some point, I would exhaust myself by uselessly spinning my wheels, and then I'd completely check out. I'd find myself either messing around on Facebook or reading ESPN. (Go Packers!)

💜 Stagnation: Often, the work I really ought to have been doing to move my business in the direction I wanted it to go - like write a blog post or record a video or work on my next book - wouldn't get done. (Actually, any sort of long-term strategy or project in what Stephen Covey used to call the "Important but Not Urgent" category would go untouched.)

At the time this was happening, I was working on what I called my inner game, which was basically my mindset. But (and this is an important "but,") *I was only focusing on the mindset strategies that revolved around making money.*

If a strategy didn't directly lead to attracting more money, I wouldn't do it. Even if I thought it sounded interesting and wanted to try it, I would tell myself I'd do it later, when I was "finally making enough money to relax."

(This of course never happened, because I wasn't doing any mindset work that would allow me to relax.)

37

So, what DID end up happening? Well, I did make more money. I broke six figures and then made multiple six figures, and I was able to sustain it.

BUT, ironically, the more money I made, the more anxious and worried I felt.

Think of it this way:

If you're a runner and you only work out your legs, will you become a better runner? Probably. Will you be healthier and in better shape?

Ummm .... probably not. (Have you seen runners who ignore their upper body? It's not really that attractive or healthy-looking.)

This is why it's SO important to work on your entire mindset - not just on the money-attraction exercises.

Not because they don't work – I can tell you firsthand they DO – but if you're stuck in fear and scarcity, there's a price to pay.

And that price is your peace of mind.

Kendra E Thornbury, Spiritual Entrepreneur and Wealth Coach (more from her in Part Three), says that creating money using fear-based emotions tends to perpetuate even more fear.

That's exactly what happened in my situation. In fact, I probably accelerated the fear, anxiety, worry and noise in my head with all my money-attraction exercises, which ultimately likely hastened my meltdown in 2012. (In retrospect, I can see how this is exactly what needed to happen in order for me to start to realize how important working on your entire mindset was - not just the money attraction stuff.)

Now, before I get into the exercises to break the hold your fear-based emotions have over you, I'd like to invite you to first shift your perspective on your fear-based emotions.

There are two steps to this process.

Step One: Consider your fear-based emotions an internal guide.

Fear-based emotions are not inherently "bad" or "evil" (despite how they might feel to you right now).

In fact, the deeper I've studied love-based and fear-based emotions, the more I've come to realize that fear-based emotions are actually a necessary part of our existence here on planet earth. They provide an important function by letting us know when something is off-track. It may be ourselves; it may be the situation; it may be the way we're handling the situation (or not handling the situation); it may be a choice we're about to make, or a choice we have made that was the wrong choice; it may be because we're missing someone we love, etc. You get the idea.

But, somehow, somewhere along the way, most of us have lost sight of the fact that our fear-based emotions are simply there to guide us and help us. Instead, we view them as things we need to NOT feel – to "get over" as quickly as possible. Or, we allow them to suck us down into a spiral of negativity ("I am a loser. I'll never amount to anything. My dad was right and I should give up on my dreams," etc.).

Instead of saying, "Oh, I feel worried right now. Let me check in and see if I need to course-correct or if I'm feeling this way because I'm stepping into something bigger," we say, "Oh, I'm so worried about money right now! Maybe I better see if I can work extra hours or take on that extra job." Or, we bury or run from our worried feelings and do something to distract or numb ourselves, like watch TV or drink or overeat or start a fight, etc.

But, if we can start to see our fear-based emotions as part of a helpful, internal guide that lets us know we're off track somewhere, it could be an important first step to stopping those emotions from controlling us.

So that's **Step One** in shifting your perspective around fear-based emotions.

Step Two: Start moving the energy of your fear-based emotions by feeling and integrating them.

When you push away or deny or numb your fear-based emotions, they tend to get trapped and stuck in your body, which not only makes it more difficult to integrate them, but it can also make you sick. (I know I'm talking a lot about fear, worry and anxiety, because that's what I personally struggled with, but this applies to any fear-based emotion, so if you're stuck in grief, depression, anger, resentment, guilt, shame, jealousy, etc. or even some combination of fear-based emotions, this applies.)

Below are five exercises that can help you start to release those fear-based emotions, and the hold they have over you.

While I want you to go through these exercises now, be sure to also add them to your "Mindset Toolbox" for the future. Pamela Bruner says this is non-negotiable – you must have at least one mindset tool like the ones below to use as you continue to grow and expand, to help you overcome obstacles as you develop. (And when you think about it, it's tough enough to up-level and/or set bigger and bolder goals, right? So why make it more difficult for yourself than it has to be?)

Also, if you haven't already, this may be a good time to download the Money and Mindset Blueprint here:

http://www.LoveBasedMoney.com/blueprint

Remember, this blueprint is designed to help you *pinpoint the best money and mindset exercises for your specific situation,* and also, to help you design your own Money and Mindset Breakthrough Plan.

Releasing Fear-Based Emotions EXERCISE One: Breathing

I have a confession:

For years, I would roll my eyes every time I heard any of the "stop and breathe" advice.

But I've recently delved into the whole breathing thing more deeply, and not only has it become my "go-to" tool every time I run into my "stuff," but I've also discovered there's a trick to it.

The trick is you need to feel your feelings.

So when uncomfortable or unpleasant thoughts come up, the idea is to pause and breathe into the emotions surrounding the unpleasant thoughts.

Remember, feelings just want to be felt. And if they're fear-based, like worry, anger, guilt, shame, anxiety, fear, etc. they're probably uncomfortable and you don't want to feel them. So, you stuff them down or run away from them or ignore them or numb them.

Alas, that doesn't actually make them go away. If you want them to go away, you need to take the time to feel them.

So, here's how this would work:

When a fear-based emotion rears its ugly head (guilt, shame, anger, grief, etc.), rather than going with your first knee-jerk reaction (starting a fight, calling a friend to gossip and/or complain about the situation, sending a very unwise email/posting a very unwise Tweet or Facebook message, pouring a glass of wine, pulling a carton of Rocky Road ice cream out of the freezer, procrastinating, watching cute cat videos on YouTube, buying things you don't need, etc.), you stop.

Just stop.

Close your eyes and breathe into that feeling.

Just feel it. Breathe into it. (And if you're a worrier like me, turn off the story in your head around it and just *feel the feeling* without the mind chatter.)

What does it mean to "breathe into it"?

For me, I feel things in my gut. That's where my worry manifests, so when I "breathe into it," I literally imagine breathing into the actual worry where it resides. I focus on it, and direct my breath into it.

You might even want to address it, mentally. Acknowledge it. Tell it you know it's there, and you feel it.

The first time you do this, you may find it very unpleasant. But if you keep it up, you'll find that it not only gets easier and easier to do, but that it also helps your blocks and resistances slowly melt away.

Now, if this is working for you, you may want to take the "advanced" course in this area: get (and follow!) Brown's book, *The Presence Process*.

The book walks you through a simple 11-week program that takes only a little over 30 minutes a day to complete. (You do a very basic breathing exercise and a little reading each day.)[3]

However, let's not confuse "simple" with "easy"!

I learned about this book about a year after I had my initial breakthrough, and as soon as I heard about it from a friend, I knew I needed to read it and go through the course. But, as these things go, I didn't actually get the book and start the program until after my mother's death in 2015. I thought it would be a good container to process my grief.

And it was. But it was also so much more. It helped me reach levels of peace and acceptance I didn't think were possible. And, with those new levels of peace, I've been able to show up for my business in a far more powerful and aligned way.

But I'll tell you, it's not for the faint of heart. It will likely test you like nothing else has (although the rewards on the other side are soooo worth it).

If you're supposed to read this book, you'll know it. You'll feel it in your gut. And I would love to encourage you to take the plunge and do it.

3   Michael Brown, *The Presence Process* (2015)

Now, if you're not ready to dive deep, it's okay! This is a process. Easing into it is MORE than okay – it's smart! Try one of the next four exercises first, and see how you feel.

Releasing Fear-Based Emotions EXERCISE Two: Byron Katie's "The Work"

If you're not familiar with Byron Katie or "The Work," I invite you to check out her website where she lays out this exercise in its entirety for free at TheWork.com. (You can also check out her books as well, if you want to go deeper than what she provides on her website.)

I'll just give you the basics here.

In a nutshell, "The Work" gives you a way to question the truth of the stories we tell ourselves.

So, let's take this one, for example:

If I make too much money, my spouse will leave me.

You would begin by writing that story - that statement - on a piece of paper, and then, you journal the answers to the following four questions:

1. Is it true? (Yes or no. If no, move to three.)

2. Can you absolutely know that it's true? (Yes or no.)

3. How do you react - what happens - when you believe that thought?

4. Who would you be without the thought?

Then, you turn around the original statement and answer the questions with the turnaround.

So, in this case, a couple of the turnarounds may be:

- ♥ If I make too much money, my spouse won't leave me.

- ♥ If I make too much money, I may leave my spouse.

(Note, the turnaround is very important, and you want to turnaround the original question a couple of times like I demonstrated here.)

"The Work" is a very powerful way to help you see the truth of what's blocking you, so you can work through those blocks.

Releasing Fear-Based Emotions EXERCISE Three: The Enneagram

Reading *The Wisdom of the Enneagram: The Complete Guide to Psychological and Spiritual Growth for the Nine Personality Types* by Don Richard Riso and Russ Hudson was the first thing I did after my meltdown in 2012.

My spiritual mentor recommended I read it, after telling me my energy was crazy (which it was). She wanted me to begin grounding myself, to take salt water baths, to meditate (which I definitely resisted and did pretty reluctantly), and to read The Enneagram.

In a nutshell, The Enneagram provides us with a way to better understand our all our wounds.[4]

There are nine personality types (I'm a six, if you're curious). Each type has a carefully-crafted response to situations, which may be either conscious or unconscious, designed to protect themselves from their worst fear. (And just to complicate things a bit more, the great cosmic joke is that the more you try and protect yourself from your greatest fear, the more you'll actually attract that fear into your life. A vicious cycle, isn't it?)

(Side note: I realize now that what I used to believe – that I had possibly created certain things in my life when I DIDN'T worry about them – was the direct opposite of what was really occurring.)

For example, let's say you fear you'll never find a relationship, and will be alone for the rest of your life. So, to keep yourself from being alone, when you are with a partner, you're so terrified he or she will leave you, you cling to him or her, and that clinging behavior ultimately drives him/her away.

---

4   Don Richard Riso and Russ Hudson *The Wisdom of the Enneagram: The Complete Guide to Psychological and Spiritual Growth for the Nine Personality Types* (1999)

The truth is, if you could just relax - stop worrying and clinging - your partner would likely stay. But you're in so much fear about him/her leaving, you can't relax, unless you're clinging.

And, of course, that cycle continues with the next relationship, because now you're even more terrified that person is going to leave you too, so you cling even more, etc.

See how that works?

I've barely scratched the surface here, but if you're interested in learning more about how your personality type responds to fear, etc., I highly encourage you to purchase and read this book.

Now, to be fair, what actually changed my life wasn't necessarily knowing my type (although that certainly explained an awful lot about myself). It was in doing the included exercise to help me break free of my behavior patterns, so I was no longer controlled by my type that started the transformation.

Here's the short version of that exercise:

When you are triggered, you must first become aware of your behavior. Then you stop that behavior, and breathe into the emotion until the trigger dissipates.

Yes, it absolutely works. And, yes, practicing it was the start of my breaking free from my worry and anxiety. (Sixes, by the way, are constant worriers. Our passion and/or vice is fear - which is ironically appropriate that I'm now writing an entire business series on how to shift from fear-based emotions to love-based. Anyway, if you too are a massive worrier, and you're ready to do the work to change it, I can't recommend this process highly enough.)

Releasing Fear-Based Emotions EXERCISE Four: Emotional Freedom Technique (EFT) a.k.a. "Tapping"

As effective as it is to simply feel your uncomfortable emotions and breathe into them in order to integrate them so they no longer trigger you, it's not the slightest bit easy. This is especially true if what you're trying to integrate is traumatic in any way. If that's the case, it may be way too difficult and painful to do it on your own.

That's where the Emotional Freedom Technique (EFT) - or "tapping" - comes in.

Tapping is a simple, self-administered acupressure technique that has been scientifically proven to calm the amygdala - the fear center of the brain. It also lowers the cortisol (stress hormone) levels in the bloodstream.

Truth be told, it looks a little silly when you're doing it (you're basically tapping parts of your body with a finger), but it's pretty remarkable how well it works!

In fact, therapists who used tapping with war veterans suffering from Post-Traumatic Stress Disorder were able to actually cure them in only a handful of sessions.

I first learned about tapping and how you could use it for business success from Pamela Bruner, Business Coach, Author, and EFT Tapping Expert. She helps entrepreneurs bust through their mindset blocks so they can grow their business. Her specialty is working through marketing and selling blocks (but you can use tapping for any sort of mindset or money block).

She explains it like this:

For many conscious and heart-centered entrepreneurs, there is a huge divide between what they do in their business (which, in many cases, is very altruistic and service-based) and marketing and selling that business.

Sales and marketing are based on financial results. The strategies that get the best financial results are celebrated the most, right?

But, if you're heart-centered, this may make you feel uncomfortable because the results that normally concern you are not money-based. You're more likely interested in how much transformation and good you're able to bring to the world.

So, either you miss out on the great sales and marketing training out there, or you turn off your heart.

Tapping is the bridge between the two. It lowers our barriers to fear so we can entertain new ideas and concepts, such as using sales and marketing to do good in the world.

Here's an example of how tapping works:

Imagine a time when you were angry at your spouse or partner, or your child. (I mean, really, really angry.)

Got it?

Okay. In that moment, when you were SO mad, it probably wasn't easy to remember how much you love him or her.

Now, of course, once you calm down, you do. But, in the heat of the moment, not only may you not remember how much you love him/her, but you may be ready to pack your bags and walk out the door and just be done with your role as a spouse/partner or parent altogether.

That's because in the heat of the moment, the anger gets in the way of other emotions, such as love.

But, if you started tapping, you would be able to calm the anger down so you could start to entertain other emotions/ideas (not only that you love the person, but that maybe listening to his/her side of the story actually wouldn't be such a bad idea).

Now, the other thing about emotions is that they can become trapped in your body. Especially those you've experienced after a traumatic event, or those you don't want to feel, so you keep stuffing them down or numbing them or running away from them.

Once they're trapped, your body does everything it can to avoid repeating that traumatic experience.

In theory, it seems like a good plan. In practice, it doesn't really work out. For one thing, your body has a difficult time distinguishing between what is actually traumatic and what isn't, especially when you're dealing with what's traumatic to a child versus an adult.

For instance, let's say you're 13 and you ask the girl or boy you have a crush on to the dance ... and that person turns you down. It's humiliating. And traumatic.

Fast forward to 33. You're with a prospective customer and you're about to ask for the sale. Your body flashes back to the 13-year-old you, and immediately thinks, "Oh no, I'm not asking again. What if she turns me down and humiliates me again?" So, you find yourself unable to ask for the sale at all, or you stumble your way through it so badly, you're absolutely sure there's no way you're getting it.

Now, to be clear, this is your body reacting to the childhood trauma - not your mind. So, you most likely aren't consciously

52

remembering your 13-year-old wounded self. What may be happening is that your mind freezes up and you can't remember anything … or you start to stutter, or maybe you decide you suck at sales and just quit doing sales calls altogether.

Here's another example:

Maybe when you were seven, you were a bee in a school play, and you tripped and fell on stage and the audience laughed. Your subconscious may have then decided it wasn't safe for you to be visible.

Fast forward to adulthood. You find yourself hiding out in a corner of every single networking event you attend, munching on veggies and cheese instead of talking to new potential connections.

You see, your conscious and unconscious mind don't really communicate. Your unconscious mind could be saying, "This networking event is dangerous. Remember how we felt when we fell down on stage? We don't want to do that again," while your conscious mind says, "I don't want to go to that networking event because it will be boring, and the food will be bad."

Pamela shared another story from a woman entrepreneur who had built her business working one-on-one with clients, and then wanted to turn her expertise into a group program so she could better leverage her time. Sounds pretty straightforward, right?

Well …

Every time she sat down to work on creating her group program, she'd hear a voice in her head saying, "Who am I to do this?" Like clockwork, she would then decide she absolutely needed to do laundry (or some other tedious task) immediately, instead.

Now, a lot of people don't hear the initial voice - they just suddenly have a strong urge to do laundry or check email or get on social media. These are all forms of procrastination, which is another sign you have a block. (It's true … if you're procrastinating on a task that could move your business or life forward, there's probably a block there.)

I started this section on tapping by talking about the divide between being a conscious business owner and the role you play in sales and marketing, but tapping can help any fear: fear of rejection, fear of being misunderstood, fear of being abandoned, fear of being ostracized or attacked - not to mention the hidden fears we aren't even aware we have.

It's no wonder so many people end up playing it safe and staying small for much (if not all) of their life, right? There is a LOT to deal with here.

(If tapping is something you'd like to learn more about - and maybe watch a demonstration of - in the Resources section, you'll find a link to a free video series where Pamela demonstrates what tapping looks like and how you can use it to get rid of your blocks.)

Releasing Fear-Based Emotions EXERCISE Five: Spring Cleaning

Melinda Cohan, Transformation Leader and Founder of The Coaches Console, shared this exercise with me (she learned it from Mama Gena). She does it daily, and it's been a key foundational piece of her success in growing a profitable software company in a short amount of time. (I have a few more exercises of hers that I share in later chapters, too.)

Spring Cleaning is designed to provide you with a safe, sacred place to "dump a charge" on a topic. What's a charge? Well, it's what happens when you get triggered by something. Maybe it's a work or family situation. Maybe it's a political argument on Facebook. It really could be anything at all - any topic that when you think about it, you find yourself getting angry or sad or worried or anxious. You get the picture.

When you're swirling around in fear-based emotions, you're far more likely to react to something happening in a negative manner. So, for instance, you have a bad day at work. You go home, start making dinner, and absolutely lose it on the kids because they are being loud in the other room.

Plus, remember that when we are triggered, we're taught to bury it, get over it, move past it, run from it etc. But the problem with burying it or trying to move past it is that we then don't feel it. (I know, I keep saying it, but feelings just want to be felt.) If we don't feel our emotions, they don't go away, no matter how deeply we try to bury them.

But, when you regularly practice Spring Cleaning, you're able to move those emotions through you, and express them, so you can truly let them go and connect to your truth and creativity.

Okay, for this exercise, you need another person. This must be a person you absolutely trust to hold what you say in strict confidence, as well as to follow the rules (yes, there are rules).

Those rules are:

- No coaching.

- No fixing.

- No bringing up whatever was said during Spring Cleaning ever again.

You also have to be careful to not let this exercise descend into a "gossip/bitch fest." All that does is feed the drama that's already happening inside you. It will NOT let you move through the emotions effectively.

Begin by setting a timer for 15 minutes. (If you both want to go through this exercise, then each person gets 15 minutes.) Now, it's possible to do this for only five minutes (and if you only have five, it's certainly better to Spring Clean for that long than to not do it at all), but the longer you go, the deeper you'll go, which gives you an opportunity to really clean out everything that's triggering you around the situation.

Here's how this works:

One person watches the timer, asks questions and holds the sacred space. The other actively Spring Cleans.

The person who is holding the space and asking the questions will start.

She says:

"Tell me about XX."

The XX is whatever is triggering you - some examples could be:

"Tell me about your business."

"Tell me about your boss."

"Tell me about your husband."

"Tell me about money."

You answer. Try and keep your response to a few statements. This will help you avoid falling into complaining and gossiping. Also, try and focus on the emotions you feel about the situation.

When you finish talking, the person holding the space will say:

"Thank you. What do you have on XX?" (The same topic as before.)

You answer again, except this time, you've been invited to dive deeper into what's really going on. So do exactly that – go deeper.

When you finish, she says again "Thank you. What do you have on XX?"

And it repeats until 15 minutes have gone by, at which point the person holding the space will say. "Your 15 minutes are up. You have three more turns. So, tell me about XX."

And, you have three more turns to complete the exercise.

As you can see, this is your chance to thoroughly talk out whatever is triggering you. The idea is to just get it out of your system. The person listening is simply holding space; she isn't getting sucked into the drama or the energy of what's going on. She isn't there to fix you or offer advice or even to agree with you. She simply holds the space while you unload.

Here's an example of how the entire process might look:

"Tell me about your boss."

"My boss is such a jerk. He gave that big project to Gina today. It should have been mine! I've been working so hard on it. I deserved it! Not Gina."

"Thank you. What do you have on your boss?"

"He does this to me all the time. He's always pulling the rug out from under me. I work and work only to see all my hard work go down the drain and someone else get rewarded."

"Thank you. What do you have on your boss?"

"When he does things like this to me, I feel invisible. Like he doesn't value anything I do. Like I don't matter."

"Thank you. What do you have on your boss?"

"When he does things like this to me, I feel like I have to work that much harder to get noticed, and I'm already so exhausted and burned-out from working so much. I don't know what to do."

And so on. You can see how each time the person holding the space asks the question, it acts as an invitation to go deeper with the answer - to really get to the heart of the matter - what's really bothering you.

As you speak to what's really going on, you're of course then feeling the specific emotions, which means the energy of that emotion is passing through you (mission accomplished!). And, as this is a safe container where you're simply "dumping the charge," it can't escalate. It won't suddenly build into a feeding frenzy of drama (which is yet another way we keep ourselves from just letting fear-based emotions move through us … we create drama around it, which keeps us from fully feeling those fear-based emotions and perpetuates the cycle).

At the end of the 15 minutes (plus three final turns), the person holding the space says: "It's been 15 minutes and that concludes our Spring Cleaning. It's been an honor to hold this sacred space for you."

Bonus Tip: Melinda likes to end with a brag, gratitude, and a desire. You'll find that exercise in Chapter Seven. This isn't required, but she highly recommends it.

So, that covers our five main exercises to help you move past your fear-based emotions. Now, there are certainly other exercises that can help you do this, but I know from my own experience that these five are highly effective, and at least one should work for everyone. If nothing else, it will help you get started integrating and moving through your fear-based emotions, and maybe that's all you need right now.

Now that we've talked about strategies to integrate fear-based emotions so you can move past them and not be controlled by them, let's move into shifting your mindset into love and abundance.

Part 2

SHIFTING YOUR MINDSET INTO LOVE AND ABUNDANCE

Chapter 4
CHANGE YOUR BRAIN, CHANGE YOUR LIFE

To recap, Part One was all about cleaning out the "crap" in your head (all the fear-based emotions - fear, worry, shame, anxiety, guilt, grief, anger) so that you are not only no longer controlled by them, but so you'll also be able to hear your intuition/inner wisdom/divine source more clearly.

Part Two is all about how you can start to shift into a mindset of love and abundance, while actually being able to listen to what your intuition/inner wisdom/divine source is saying to you, so you can follow it.

But, before I get into all of that, let me give you a little background about how the brain works.

I'm not planning on getting real technical here (I'm not a doctor or scientist), but I want to share some basic information to give you a better understanding about how (and WHY) all this mindset stuff works.

What you think of as your mind is what's considered your conscious mind. It's where your ego hangs out, and it's the smallest part of your brain.

The much larger part of your brain (over 90%) is your unconscious mind. This is the part of the mind that, among other things, controls your automatic bodily functions, like your heartbeat and digestion. It's also where your intuition and creativity live, as well as where you go when you dream.

It's also the part of you that keeps you safe and houses your core beliefs.

Why is that important? Because that's where all your blocks reside, too.

You see, if you have a mindset block around making money, then you're never going to make more money. Your subconscious will make sure you don't.

How does it do that?

You get sick before a meeting with a huge potential client. (Remember, your subconscious controls your bodily functions and can certainly turn on the cold and flu symptoms if it so desires.) You procrastinate and never find time to do what's really calling you on a soul level – like starting a business, writing a book, etc. You get distracted with worry or fear or gossip or anger and end up not doing the things you need to be doing to make more money, such as marketing your business.

You get the picture.

Now, along with mindset blocks, you also develop "grooves" in the neural pathways in your brain. In fact, a lot of habits are formed from these grooves.

These grooves make living our lives much easier, because we don't have to consciously think about every little thing we do. (Can you imagine having to think through brushing your teeth every day?)

The problem is, these grooves can also prevent us from living the life we desire. If we have habits that aren't supporting the life we desire, then it's going to be very difficult (if not impossible) to create that life. And, if you have a self-sabotage groove, then you're going to consistently self-sabotage.

(What's a self-sabotage groove? Well, for instance, is there something negative in your life that keeps happening to you, even though you don't want it to? Yeah, that's probably a self-sabotage groove.)

Another way to think about grooves is to imagine rolling a big rock into the middle of a stream. The water will naturally flow around the rock, and if it's there long enough, it can actually change the current of the stream. The water will always flow where there's the least resistance.

The grooves in your brain are the pathways of least resistance.

What all of this means is that part of what we're doing in this section is actually rewiring the brain. We're getting out of those grooves.

The exercises in this section are designed to bust through blocks, build new neural pathways, or both.

One easy way to start rewiring your brain (both to eliminate blocks and to get rid of those self-sabotage grooves) is to start a meditation practice.

Now, for everyone out there who is right now protesting "No way! I tried to meditate and it doesn't work for me," or "I don't have time to meditate," just take a moment to breathe.

Breathe, and listen. ☺

First off, if you really are against meditating, then don't meditate. I'm not here to force you to do anything you don't want to.

All I'm asking is for you to keep reading, and to keep an open mind.

Let's start by discussing meditation in general.

Perform a Google search on "the benefits of meditation," and article after article will pop up. There is no doubt that meditation improves your health. It has been shown to slow the heart rate and breathing pace, reduce the body's response to pain, decrease stress/fear levels, increase focus, creativity, and happiness, improve self-esteem and general life outlook, deepen spiritual connection, and more.

Meditation can also start to melt away mindset blocks and make it easier to get out of those well-worn, self-sabotaging grooves.

Okay, so meditation is good for you. We can agree on that, right?

Yet so are a lot of things, like exercise and flossing and drinking green drinks … and many times, we simply don't do the things that are good for us regularly, even though we know they're good for us.

So what makes meditation different? Why am I encouraging you to power through your resistance to do it?

Because not only does it provide all the benefits I listed above, but it also quiets the mind and allows your brain to form new neural pathways that don't lead to your blocks. And the more you do it, the greater the results you experience.

Now, when you think of the word "meditation," you probably instantly get an image of sitting completely still on the floor, in silence, for 30 minutes or longer.

While yes, that IS a form of meditation, it isn't the only one.

What if there was another way to meditate that would allow you to enjoy all the juicy benefits?

Luckily, there is. (There's actually quite a few ways.)

Studies have indicated that just stopping a few times a day for a couple of minutes to do some deep breathing exercises is more beneficial than meditating straight for a 20 to 30-minute chunk of time. So, one option is to stop for just a few minutes at a time, a few times throughout your day, to control your breathing.

Or maybe you try a walking meditation, which adds the benefit of exercise too, so you're essentially accomplishing two things at once (both of which you know you should be doing more of, right?). Now, this one is a little different than a more standard meditation, because first and foremost, your eyes are open, and you're moving. The thing is, meditation is an INNER process. So even though your eyes are open and you're moving, the key is to still focus on the inner process. Here, you focus on the physical, mental, and emotional experiences of walking as the foundation of developing awareness. It's about mindfulness. It's about learning to keep your focus from all outer distraction, while you go inward.

Or, maybe you try my favorite: meditations with audio (see the Resources section to get some of the ones I like and use the most). And by the way, I don't sit on a hard floor where I'm miserable the whole time. I make myself super-comfortable with pillows, and I just listen. Some are guided meditations - some just play soothing meditation music.

Basically, as long as you're doing something to quiet your mind and live in the present moment, even if it only lasts for a minute, you're golden. Remember, meditation is called a PRACTICE, and you are definitely PRACTICING.

This means that some days, you'll be so "in the flow" you'll feel like you're practically levitating, while other days, you may not be able to get your mind to quiet down to save your life. Or you fall asleep, and drool all over yourself. ;)

Guess what? That's okay too.

What's important here is that you're actually showing up, and practicing. It WILL get easier if you stick with it, and regardless of how messy or completely unproductive it might feel, you'll still get the benefits.

I know this because for years, I couldn't meditate either.

I couldn't quiet my mind. All I could do was think about my to-do list - all the things I knew I had to get done and how much time I was wasting just sitting there.

But, when I finally started listening to the meditation tapes, everything changed. It gave me something else to focus on instead of all the things I thought needed my attention RIGHT THAT MINUTE. (At least, that's what my conscious mind kept telling me.)

Plus, the tapes give me something to focus when my mind does wander, so I can bring my attention back.

There are SO many types of meditation (and ways to meditate) that chances are high you can find something that would work for you.

If nothing else, you could simply take 10-15 minutes to lay down to just relax and breathe.

Other ideas for releasing blocks and rewiring your brain:

✔ Yoga: With a big focus on breathing, yoga also provides the obvious exercise benefits, too (yet another good choice if you're a multi-tasker).

✔ Epsom Salt Baths: The salts literally pull the emotions and energy out of your body and into the water. It's also a great way to add some relaxation and meditation into your day. Light a candle, play some meditation or relaxation tapes, and you've got a great ritual you can keep repeating to help shift your mindset into love and abundance.

✔ Grounding: Go outside and stand on the ground with your bare feet (obviously this isn't going to work all that well in the winter months, especially if you live somewhere that actually has a winter). When you stand outside with your bare skin touching the earth, you can literally "ground" yourself in the earth, and discharge fear-based energy into it.

Right after my meltdown, my spiritual mentor told me to stand outside every day and listen to three songs I loved. I did this faithfully every morning for about three months (most of the time with the sun shining on me as well) and it really made a big difference in helping me clear the worry and fear-based emotions from inside me, so I could start to function again.

EXERCISE: Daily Practice

One of the habits successful people often share is something called a daily practice.

For the most part, successful people don't wait until the last second to roll out of bed and frantically begin their day. They tend to get up earlier, so they can spend some time setting themselves up to have a successful day.

This is called a daily practice.

Daily practices vary greatly but they typically include:

- Some type of meditation practice. This can vary from a breathing and visualization practice (where you take a few minutes and visualize your day), to a typical 20-60-minute meditation.

- A gratitude practice (more on that later).

- Affirmations (more on that later).

💗 Journaling (more on that in the next chapter).

💗 Reading - personal development or spiritual development books are a favorite, but sometimes nonfiction or informational reading has the same effect.

💗 Some sort of physical movement, whether it be yoga or a walk or a full-out exercise routine.

💗 Prayer, or some other form of connecting to God/Source/ Universe. (For instance, maybe you pick an angel card/ tarot card, or you practice directed writing where you have a conversation with God on paper, or chant.)

💗 Visualization - maybe you visualize how you want your day to go, or you see yourself reaching a specific goal, or getting a check in the mail.

💗 A combination of the above (pretty much everyone I know who has a daily practice typically combines some of the above).

Now, did you notice what ISN'T included in this list? Checking email. Updating social media. Getting yourself or your family ready to leave the house. Jumping into any sort of to-do list.

The daily practice happens BEFORE your day officially starts. It's a quiet time for you to get connected to your dreams, goals, higher self, God, etc. It's to get yourself grounded, raise your vibration (more on that in the next chapter) and to set yourself up for a successful, productive day.

Now, let's flip this around and look at what happens if you don't have a daily practice.

Maybe you grab your smart phone or flip open your laptop to check your email, sometimes even before going to the bathroom. (Yep, this was me for many, many years.)

Maybe your mornings are a chaotic mess, where you're trying to get yourself or your family (or both) ready for the day, and it's filled with nagging or fighting or other unpleasantness.

Either way, if you start your day without a daily practice, you likely start your day either in your own drama or in other people's energy (which means you're focusing on their drama or needs first). Regardless, how you want your day to unfold is an afterthought.

Which also likely means that all those goals and dreams - the ones Stephen Covey calls "important but not urgent" (which are things that are really important to you but have no urgent deadline, like writing your book or doing your art or starting your business or working ON your business versus IN your business or finally getting in shape) - never get done.

If you don't regularly connect to what's important to you, you probably won't make space to regularly work on those "important but non-urgent" things. And, I hate to be the one to break it to you, but if that's the case, they're just not going to get done.

But, that's not the worst part of not having a daily practice.

You see, without a daily practice, you're also likely starting your day drowning in fear-based emotions.

Take a moment now and think about your typical morning. Focus on your emotions, rather than HOW you start day.

How are you FEELING? Exhausted? Frantic? Resentful? Angry? Overwhelmed? Frustrated? Taken advantage of? Out of control? All of the above?

These are textbook fear-based emotions.

And, when you start your day feeling those fear-based emotions, all you're doing is putting yourself behind the eight ball.

You'll have to exert a bunch of energy just to get back to neutral, much less shift to love and abundance (if you're even able to).

But when you start your day with a daily practice, you begin your day with love-based emotions instead. Even if your morning is still crazy and lowers your initial good feelings, you won't be as low as you would be without your daily practice. Plus, you'll likely be able to recover faster and get back to high level pretty quickly.

Now, if you're anything like me, you may be resisting right now. I so get it.

When I first heard about a daily practice, I definitely resisted. I didn't have time. I didn't like getting up early in the morning. And if I couldn't check my email right away, I was filled with so much anxiety and worry that I'd practically make myself sick.

Let's talk about these resistances, because I have a feeling you might experience them too.

Yes, I'm going to recommend you get up earlier to do your daily practice. Ideally, 30 minutes earlier, but if that makes you feel like throwing this book across the room and running away screaming, start with 15.

If you can't even manage that, take a few minutes to do a gratitude exercise while still lying in bed. (You'll find one in Chapter Seven, courtesy of Elizabeth Purvis, Creatrix, Feminine Magic® and Founder of Goddess Business School.)

Now, getting up early isn't the only option. If you have flexibility in your schedule, you absolutely could rearrange your morning routine to incorporate a daily practice.

I have a good friend who is a mother of very young children and an entrepreneur, and while she does start her day by getting her kids and husband ready for theirs, she does her daily practice right after that, and before jumping into email and her business to-do list. So, play with shifting your morning routine around a bit to see if you can figure out something that fits your lifestyle, because the more it does, the easier it'll be for you to make it a habit.

And if you're committed to shifting your mindset and attracting more abundance into your life, incorporating a morning practice should be a piece of cake.

No excuses - right?

Well …

I have a secret to share with you.

If I had been sitting where you are any time before my meltdown in November 2012, there's no way I would have done any of this.

Never would have happened. Not even the little gratitude exercise while I was still in bed.

It wouldn't have been for lack of trying. Or lack of pushing myself. Or lack of turning my willpower into a battering ram to force myself to do this work.

I may have done something for a few days, maybe even a week or two. But, eventually, I would have just petered out and stopped altogether. Things would have come up; I'm sure of it. In my case, it would likely be client work that just "had" to be done before my daily practice. (Priorities, right? ;)

Of course if I started out with client work, I would never circle back to my daily practice. And, for me, it truly wasn't physically *possible* to do anything other than check email first thing. If I didn't, I would have been so consumed with anxiety and worry about what was waiting for me in my inbox that I wouldn't have been able to focus on anything else.

Of course, now I clearly see what the real problem was. My head was a train wreck - full of noise and confusion and worry and anxiety, and my inner critic was constantly yammering at me for one thing or another. I spent most of my life trying to relieve the pressure in my head, which meant doing things like obsessively checking my email or obsessively having a couple of glasses of wine a night or obsessively working out (for most of 2012 leading up to my meltdown, I started exercising more and more until I was going to the gym six to seven times a week for intense and challenging workouts - which I grant you wasn't necessarily a bad habit like the obsessive email checking or wine drinking, but I was certainly on a path to over-exercising).

My ego had such a death grip on me I could barely breathe. I couldn't possibly make space for anything like a daily practice. Looking back now, I'm amazed I got anything done at all.

What finally broke this hectic way of life for me was everything that happened after the meltdown: forcing myself to slow down, breathe, feel my emotions (rather than stuffing or numbing). Shutting down the story in my head so I was simply breathing into my emotions, by doing things like the breathing exercise I outlined in Part One.

Once all the noise, worry, and anxiety quieted down and I had peace in my head, I discovered I could actually start - and maintain - a daily practice.

First, I started getting up with the sun at 5:30 a.m. (yes, you read that right). Keep in mind this is from a woman who for years thought getting up at eight a.m. was a massive hardship. (In college, the 8:50 am class was, like, ridiculously early and I would typically spend my entire semester cursing that class.) I never considered myself a morning person. But, I've come to realize that the early morning hours are the best time to work on my own books, and since writing my books is important to me, I now drag myself out of bed as the sun wakes me up.

Believe it or not, it's not nearly as bad as I thought it would be.

Because I'm up so early, I have time to write my books, sit quietly and stare out the window with my coffee or tea, meditate, walk my dog, make breakfast for everyone, and take a shower before I get "officially" started with emails and phone calls and to-do lists.

I'm sharing my story with you because I believe a daily practice can change your life.

And if you're anything like me, I want you to know that sheer willpower is only going to get you so far.

I also believe in setting yourself up for success. If you're committed to a daily practice, take some time to think about your schedule and your habits and figure out the best time for you to incorporate your daily practice into your daily life.

Now, you may be one of the lucky ones. Maybe you'll be able to jump right into a daily practice with no problems. But, if you discover you're not able to actually put a daily practice into place despite your best efforts, you may first need to work on the emotions and blocks that are stopping you (and, if this is you, it's absolutely nothing to be ashamed of). A good place to start is with the five exercises in Chapter Three that will help you move through your fear-based emotions.

Okay, so now that you know why having a daily practice is so important, you may be wondering what you should actually be doing.

I encourage you to try a few things out from the list above, and see what resonates with you. You may want to try a combination of things, such as meditating and then working out, or rotating what you do, by trying different meditation practices, or maybe journaling instead or meditating.

The Money and Mindset Blueprint at

http://www.LoveBasedMoney.com/blueprint

can also help you design a daily practice that is perfect for you.

Remember, at the end of the day, it's really about what works for you.

.

Chapter 5
CHAGEN YOUR BELIEFS, CHANGE YOUR LIFE

In the last chapter, I shared how changing your brain is the first step to changing your life.

Well, along with changing your brain, you also need to change your beliefs. In fact, changing your beliefs is crucial if you really want to see big results in your life.

So, let's start by defining "beliefs."

Beliefs are statements or stories that we consider truths.

Examples of beliefs include:

- I'm a healthy person.

- I'm always getting sick.

- I'm surrounded by a community of family and friends who love me.

- I've never been lucky in love.

- Making money is easy for me.

- Making money is difficult for me.

81

💜 I have great parking lot karma.

💜 Someone ALWAYS pulls into a space before I can.

💜 I always win raffle prizes.

💜 I never win anything.

A quick note:

If right now you're thinking, "Michele, wait! Some of those sound more like facts than beliefs. Like, 'I'm always getting sick.' How is that a belief?"

Well, remember what I shared earlier about how your health is directly related to your subconscious. So if you have a belief that you aren't healthy, your mind will look for evidence to prove you aren't healthy, and you end up getting sick.

See how that works?

Okay, so as you can see, beliefs can be positive or negative. They can be "small" beliefs and have a minimal impact on your life, or they can be "big" beliefs, and have a huge impact.

Positive beliefs – those that move your life forward in a positive way – are probably those you don't give much thought to, because they don't represent problems in your life. It's the negative beliefs that are the issue ... especially the ones that hold you back from what you really want.

And, if they're "hidden" negative beliefs - i.e. you're not even aware you have them - it makes it even more challenging to deal with them effectively.

(By the way, negative beliefs are synonymous with mindset blocks. You could actually re-read Chapter Four and replace "mindset blocks" with "negative beliefs"- they are the same.)

Eva Gregory, Founder of Leading Edge Coaching & Training, LLC., is a mindset expert who specializes in helping spiritual entrepreneurs get past their money blocks and make more money. According to her, 90-95% of your success comes from your mindset: more specifically, from the beliefs we have.

And if our beliefs are limiting, we need to shift them.

She has a Mindset Mastery Formula, which looks like this:

thought (belief) + emotional charge + action = outcome

So, here's how this works:

You have a thought or a belief. This thought or belief creates a feeling (or emotional charge), which then determines the action you take or don't take, which of course results in the outcome.

Okay, so let's take a look at an example at what this looks like in the real world:

Let's say you're an entrepreneur who wants to grow your business, and you have a belief that it isn't safe to be visible. (Or, another way to look at it is you have a fear of being seen or a fear of being visible.)

So, one day, you get an email inviting you to speak at a really big conference in your industry. Initially you're super-excited; this is your big break! You're going to speak in front of a room full of your ideal prospects who will *finally* hear your message (not to mention hopefully choose to work with you).

Of course, if you're on stage, you're going to be seen. And, you have a fear around being seen, which means after the initial excitement wears off, fear may creep in and take serious hold.

(Note: This limiting belief may not be obvious. In fact, it likely won't be. You won't suddenly realize "I have a fear of being seen." It will probably feel more like this: "Am I *ready* for this? Who am I to be on a stage? Maybe they won't like me. I look fat. I need to lose 15 pounds. Maybe I'll have terrible stage fright and embarrass myself.")

Now, you may decide you're going to push through the fear with willpower. Just know that this doesn't always work. Remember, your subconscious is pretty powerful. So, maybe you "forget" to email back to accept the speaking gig, and by the time you figure

84

out the email didn't go out, you've lost the opportunity. Or, you do accept it, but you end up getting sick or you subconsciously create drama in your life or business so you have to cancel. Or, you procrastinate putting your talk together, so you end up staying up all night, and then bomb the talk, thus ensuring nothing will come out of your being seen.

Okay, so let's break this down in terms of Eva's formula.

thought/belief (it's not safe to be seen) + emotional charge (fear) + action (procrastinate sending the email or getting the talk written/ create drama/get sick) = outcome (not being seen/not growing business/not making money/not transforming lives)

The result of that uncomfortable emotional charge around that limiting thought or belief is that you either don't take any action (i.e. procrastinate or make excuses), or you don't take the right action to ensure that speaking opportunity is a success (i.e. staying up all night so you're exhausted when you finally get on the stage), which means the end result will not be what you want.

Now, this may sound overly-simplistic to you. Maybe you think you've been in situations before where you did take all the action you could have, but you still didn't get the results. Or, maybe there were some really good reasons that stopped you from taking action. Or, maybe you're not even sure what action you should or shouldn't take have taken, so you were unclear as to what you should have been doing to get the results you want.

So, first off, can you really be sure you took ALL the action you were supposed to? Every single one? Or were there a few (or more) you let slide?

And, did you do the best job you possibly could? Or did you cut a few corners? Or maybe what you did was out-and-out sloppy?

If you really get quiet and honest with yourself, you may discover you didn't actually do *everything* you could have done to get the results you wanted.

Now, let's look at some of those "good" reasons that stopped you: you got sick, a loved one got sick, some work emergency cropped up, your high school teenager got caught shoplifting.

You didn't have any control over it, so how could it be your fault?

Well …

This one may be a bit more difficult to wrap your head around, so stay with me here.

I'm not saying there aren't times in your life where you simply have to drop everything to deal with something. But, if you start noticing a pattern in your life, such as every time you take a step toward starting your own business, you get sick/your kids act up/your car acts up/etc., it may be the way your subconscious is distracting you from starting your business.

Yes, I know. This all sounds terribly "woo woo" and not at all based in reality.

But what if I were to tell you that *YOU actually create your own reality?*

(I know. This is just getting stranger by the moment, right? Just keep sticking with me. Really - it will be worth it.)

You may have heard the saying "What you focus on expands." Simplified, what this really means is that your reality is created by the way your brain filters information.

This is exactly why two people will never describe the same life event the same way.

Imagine two people sitting outside by the lake in the sunshine. One person describes a relaxing, beautiful day. The other describes a hot, uncomfortable day spent being eaten alive by bugs.

What you are focused on in your life will be reflected back to you.

There is also a school of thought that says you create whatever happens in your life. So, let's say your refrigerator suddenly goes on the fritz. There could be a lot of reasons why that happened (some sort of deeper lesson or an "Upper Limit" problem, more on that below), but most definitely one of those reasons could be that it acts as a distraction from starting your business. Now, because you need to buy a new fridge, you suddenly don't have the money you were planning on investing in your business, not to mention you just lost a bunch of time you could have used to work on your business, because you had to deal with this problem.

An important perspective to note here: If you didn't have any blocks to starting your business, it wouldn't matter if your fridge went out - you would still find a way to start your business. People have accomplished extraordinary things in the face of seemingly insurmountable challenges, so really, it's less about what life throws at you and more about how you respond to it. If you allow a broken fridge to derail you, you're allowing the "can't start a business" block to manifest itself in your life. Make sense? And, if you are recognizing yourself here - please don't beat yourself up or try and force your way through it. It won't work. Instead, use the exercises in this book to dissolve or integrate the blocks.

Okay, let's sum all this up:

- 💜 If you have a limiting belief in your subconscious, let's say around starting your own business, your subconscious will likely stop you when you begin taking steps toward starting your business.

- 💜 The way your subconscious stops you may take on many forms, but the end result will likely be that you either take no action, or the wrong action. So, in this case, you never start your own business because you either procrastinate on the things you need to do to start your business, or you take the wrong actions altogether.

💜 Some of the ways your subconscious stops you include: getting distracted when you sit down to work (maybe you feel like you need to go do the laundry or you simply don't feel like working on a specific task so you put it aside), getting sick, or having some sort of drama pop up that you "must" deal with instead.

💜 Because you never seem to find the time start your own business, you start to focus on statements like, "I never have the time to work on my business," or, "Maybe I'm just not meant to start a business," or on questions like, "Why does this always happen to me?" or, "Why am I so unlucky that I can't start a business?"

💜 Those statements feed that limiting belief and make it even stronger. So then, not only is it even more anchored in your subconscious, but you also consciously begin to perceive how your life is set up to keep you from working on your business, which of course will keep you from working on your business. Instead of seeing time and opportunities to work on your business, you'll see only excuses and reasons to stop you from doing so.

💜 You start to create a "story" around your lack of success in this area. Now, what do I mean by story?

A story is something we make up to explain a series of events in our life. For instance, "I never have time to work on my business" turns into "Well, my kids are still pretty young and they need me and my husband doesn't have the patience to deal with them in the evening, and I can't possibly quit my job because we need the money so I guess I just have to settle for not starting my business."

All of this certainly sounds true, right? Understandable.

But it's really just a set of assumptions we make. And it's entirely possible that none of them are true.

Your kids may very well benefit from you starting a business, because they would get to learn firsthand what it takes to be an entrepreneur. Your husband may not only find the patience required, but actually treasure the time he spends alone with the kids while you work for a few hours on your business. And, maybe you could quit - have you crunched the numbers? Or, maybe if you asked your boss, you could drop down to half time.

All of us have stories about lots of things - from why our friend never texted us back (we could be sitting there sure our friend is mad at us and we're spending hours spinning around trying to figure out why, when in reality, she just dropped her phone in the toilet) to why our teenager stumbled in the door completely intoxicated ("His father was always too lax with him and let him get away with murder"). Needless to say, these stories very rarely reflect the truth of the situation. Yet, we can become quite attached to them ... so much so that they start to define our reality.

What makes all of this even worse is that our stories are nearly impossible for us to see ourselves. To us, they feel like truth - so we don't question them. However, the only way we can actually unravel them IS by questioning them. (Ah, one of those little ironic jokes the Universe loves to play on us - the one thing we MUST do to break the spell is also the one thing that is practically invisible to us, which makes it feel nearly impossible to do.)

So, going back to limiting belief around starting a business:

You start to create a story around why you can't start a business - a story that may sound so truthful you don't believe it possibly COULD be a story - but regardless, that story is now feeding into that limiting belief.

And, the more you feed that limiting belief with stories and statements, the stronger that belief is going to become, which of course makes it more and more difficult to uproot the darn thing and send it packing.

See how all of this fits together?

Let's look at another example.

You'd like to start making more money. Maybe you really want to make six figures a year, but you've been hovering around the $50,000 mark for what seems like forever.

Okay, so if there seems to be a "ceiling" on what you earn every year - and no matter what you do, you can't seem to break that ceiling - you probably have some sort of financial block in your subconscious that's keeping you stuck at a level ($50K in this example). You also probably have some sort of Upper Limit problem.

The Upper Limit phrase/concept was coined by Gay Hendricks, Ph.D in the book *The Big Leap*.While Upper Limit problems are synonymous with mindset blocks, they're actually a special kind of mindset block.[5]

Basically, once you hit your "upper limit" - no whatever it is: love, creativity, health, money, joy - you end up sabotaging yourself to bring yourself back down to your "normal" level/limit.

In the case of money, if your upper limit is anything above $50,000, you'll never actually make above $50,000. If you come close, you'll find yourself getting sick or experiencing some type of drama. *Something* will stop you from getting beyond your upper limit. If it's love, it may look like you have a real breakthrough in closeness and connection with your spouse … and then five minutes later, you get into a huge fight. (If you want to learn more about the Upper Limit problem and how this may be holding you

---

5   Gay Hendricks, PH.D, *The Big Leap* (2010)

back in multiple areas of your life, I highly recommend you get the book.)

So, let's see how this all fits together when you're trying to break six figures:

* You have a mindset block and/or an Upper Limit problem when it comes to exceeding $50,000 a year, even though you really want to be making over $100,000.

* These blocks could take many forms. Maybe you get sick or distracted when you get close to making $50,000. Or if you do make over $50,000, some financial emergency pops up, so you don't actually get any sort of benefit for making the "extra" money.

* Because it doesn't seem to matter what you do, you just can't crack that ceiling. You start to focus on thoughts like:

"What's wrong with me?"

"I guess I'll always be broke."

"I'm unlucky with money."

"Why is making money so easy for so-and-so, and so difficult for me?"

"Maybe my gifts/expertise isn't all that great after all."

"I'm a loser."

"Rich people are greedy and mean."

* Along with creating statements/having thoughts around not being able to crack the $50,000 ceiling, you also create all sorts of stories as to why you can't make more money, and why all of the money-attraction exercises in the world won't work for you.

* Those statements and stories feed that limiting belief and make it even stronger. So now, not only is that belief even more anchored in your subconscious, but you are also consciously starting to perceive how your life is set up so you'll never make more than $50,000, no matter what you do or how hard you try, which of course will keep you stuck at $50,000. Instead of seeing time and opportunities to make more money (and mind you, not all of those opportunities may be work related), you'll see only excuses and reasons that stop you.

Okay, so now that you see how your mindset feeds into the results you're experiencing, the next question (and most important one) is how can you turn it all around?

One very powerful strategy I recommend is called a **pattern interrupt**.

Basically, if you're stuck in a pattern - any sort of pattern - doing something to interrupt that pattern is the first step toward breaking it.

So, for instance, you have a pattern around worrying about money. Instead of doing what you always do when you worry, something (either an internal or external stimulus) causes you to break that pattern.

An example of an internal stimulus would be noticing you're worrying. The simple act of noticing causes the pattern interrupt.

However, this is definitely not always easy to do. So, another way to interrupt the pattern is to have an external stimulus do it for you.

One tool Eva Gregory recommends is an app called the Mindfulness Bell (if you do a search, a variety of apps pop up - some free, some paid).

The Mindfulness Bell can be set to go off every hour, or it can be set to chime randomly.

The idea is that, whenever you hear the little chimes, you stop what you're doing, take a few deep breaths, and re-focus on the present.

It's a great way to incorporate an external pattern interrupt to remind you to get out of the craziness of your mind (and any fear-based emotions that are driving you), and to tune in to the present.

Another powerful strategy for keeping your mindset from feeding into your limiting beliefs is one that is designed to help you start to "see" your stories.

Whenever you feel yourself start to descend into some sort of worrying or complaining session, start out by identifying the story.

Say, "I have a story around XX."

Here's how this looks:

> "I have a story around the idea that when I get on stage, all anyone is going to see is how fat I've gotten."
>
> "I have a story around when my husband doesn't put his dishes in the dishwasher, even though I'm constantly nagging him to, it means he doesn't love me or respect me."
>
> "I have a story around how when my friend doesn't call me to go out, I feel I always have to make the first move, and she secretly doesn't like hanging out with me."
>
> "I have a story around if I don't stay in this job I hate, my family will be disappointed in me and I'll be letting everyone down."

You see where I'm going with this.

Basically what this will do is help you start to "see" the stories you tell yourself that are keeping you trapped in your fear-based emotions. Because, when you DON'T identify the stories, in a lot of cases what ends up happening is exactly what we DON'T want: our relationships are destroyed, we never follow our dreams, we do things we don't want to do, and eventually, we may end up in a life we really don't want.

For instance:

- ♥ You turn down speaking opportunities even though it's your dream to be a successful speaker.

- ♥ Your relationship with your husband deteriorates because rather than sharing with him how you're really feeling, you're picking fights and are full of resentment.

- ♥ You stop calling your friend and end up losing the friendship.

- ♥ You stay in a job you hate, and because your stress level is so high, you end up with significant health problems. Worst of all, you never pursue your dreams.

That's why learning to identify your stories so you aren't trapped by them is so crucial.

Back in 2005, when I initially decided I must be the reason I was stuck at $50,000 a year, I immediately jumped into all the different money-attraction and Law of Attraction exercises I could find (and which I've made available to you in Part Three of this book).

And, while that strategy did work, I wouldn't necessarily recommend it. The price I paid to break six figures was pretty darn high. (Note: One of my featured experts in this book, Anastasia Netri, Transformational Coach for Awakening Women, believes (and I wholeheartedly agree) that if you ARE struggling with money right now, the anxiety/worry/fear won't go away when you start making more money. In fact, it will probably get worse - partly because the fear changes from "I'm not making enough" to "I'm still not making enough AND I might lose what I made." You may not believe that right now, but I'm going to give it the old college try and see if I can convince you otherwise.)

This is why I purposefully put the book together in the order I did. I started with exercises designed to help you integrate your fear-based emotions. Then we move into transforming any beliefs that aren't serving you, and that are holding you back from what you truly desire. Finally, we cover the actual money-attraction exercises.

Keep in mind if you're filled with fear or anger or grief or shame or guilt (or all of the above along with any other fear-based emotion), anything you try in this book is going to be more difficult than it has to be. It's more difficult to quiet your mind so you can hear your inner guidance/intuition; it's more difficult to not get caught up in your stories, and it's more difficult to keep your energy vibration high (more on that in the next chapter).

Once you've cleared the crap out of your head (so to speak) then it's much easier to start to benefit from the money-attraction exercises in the next section.

And to help you clear out the crap in your head, I've put together some loose guidelines around exercises that may work for you, depending on your current biggest problems.

EXERCISE: Begin Creating a Money and Mindset Breakthrough Plan

If you haven't already, now is definitely a good time to download the Money and Mindset Blueprint at

http://www.LoveBasedMoney.com/blueprint

This blueprint will further assist you in designing your own Money and Mindset Breakthrough Plan.

In a nutshell, a Money and Mindset Breakthrough Plan should include:

- What you want your reality to look like

- What belief (or beliefs) you're focused on shifting

- What actions you are going to take to shift that belief

In addition, it should also include daily activities (i.e. your daily practice), and at least one money-attraction exercise (you can find those exercises in Part Three).

Now, if you're not sure which beliefs you should focus on shifting, or if you're feeling overwhelmed (like there are too many beliefs to focus on, or you know the beliefs you should be focusing on, but you're not sure what the right actions to take are), you may want to do some journaling too, and be sure to see Chapter Eight for a journaling exercise designed to help you identify the root cause of your money challenges.

Typically, when you're not taking steps to move yourself toward your goal, you have some sort of combination of story and limiting beliefs/fear-based emotions going on. If you find that your story is focused on what's not working (and, in this case, your story could be excuses or "I always" or "I never" statements that are just vibrating in your head), you may want to work on clarifying what's going on with your story first.

Wondering how?

Well, for me, when I'm trying to untangle stories or excuses in my head, the most beneficial exercises are journaling-related. Byron Katie's "The Work" that I talked about in Chapter Three is a perfect place to start, but you also can just write, free-form style.

And, if you're not sure where to start or exactly what is stopping you, writing is a great way to get clarity and figure out what your next steps should be, or where you should focus your energy.

Here are a few tips to make your journaling time as powerful as possible (I've also included a few different journaling exercises you can try, depending on how structured you want to be about it. You may also consider incorporating journaling into your daily practice).

Journaling Tips

1. Light a candle. (This is a ritual, remember?) Part of my ritual is to select the right candle for the mood I'm in, or what I'm trying to accomplish.

2. Gather some paper and pens or an actual journal. I'm a big believer in handwriting when you're journaling, as opposed to typing. There's something about the connection between the pen and paper that allows you to access deeper levels of your subconscious and creativity that I don't believe you get to when you're typing on a keyboard.

3. Set a timer (optional). Many journaling practices either encourage you to journal for a set amount of time, or for a set number of pages. If you're going the timer route, 20 minutes is what is typically encouraged.

4. Select some music (optional). For myself, I choose classical music from the Baroque Period: either Bach or Handel or Vivaldi. There's something about Baroque music that allows us to access deeper levels of our brain, but if you really don't like classical music, try whatever works for you. Meditation music works well here, too.

5. Select a journaling structure. Here are some ideas (but these aren't the only ones - feel free to use whatever is calling you or just make one up):

💜 Begin writing whatever comes into your head - without stopping or correcting what you write - for either a set amount of time or a set number of pages. In Julia Cameron's The Artist's Way, she talks about a practice called "morning pages," where you basically fill three pages of journaling every morning. Another practice I've seen work is to simply start writing, and to keep going until you start accessing "the gold," even if you end up writing "I don't know what to write" over and over. (Eventually you WILL find something to journal about. The key is to just keep the pen moving until you do.)[6]

💜 Structure your journaling using inquires. The brain actually responds really well to questions - if you ask a question, your brain will ponder it and toss it around until it figures out an answer.

---

6   Julia Cameron, *The Artist's Way* (2016)

However, there is one very big drawback to this: If you don't ask the right question, you won't get the right answer.

Consider this - you ask your subconscious, "Why aren't I successful yet?" Your brain mulls that about and tosses back the answer "Because you're not ready," which isn't a terribly helpful answer. (Or, even worse, maybe your inner critic gets involved and answers "Because you're a loser," which not only isn't a terribly helpful answer, but it can also make you feel bad and bring your energy way down, which will likely prevent you from getting to the right answer.)

A better question may be "What action am I being called to do next in order to be successful?" Chances are you'll get an answer that will actually help you become more successful.

This book is full of inquiries you can use in your journaling. All you need to do is pick a question, write it at the top of your journaling page, and off you go.

* God writing. Now, if God is a charged word for you, take a deep breath. It doesn't have to be "God." You can use Source, Universe, Divine, Higher Power, Inner Wisdom … whatever works for you. The point is to have a conversation on paper that allows you to access your higher self/divine wisdom.

So, how this works is to first write your name or "Me," and put a colon after it. Then ask your question. Next, write your word for God with a colon, and then the answer you receive to the question.

So, it looks something like this (and yes, I've used God, not only because God is the word I personally use, but also because it's shorter).

> Me: Are you there, God?
>
> God: Yes, my child, I'm always here.
>
> Me: I'm feeling stuck right now. What should I do to make more money?
>
> God: What do you think you should be doing?
>
> Me: Well, I know I need to be writing an email to go out, but I'm not sure what the angle should be. What do you think the angle should be?
>
> God: What would connect with your readers the most?

You get the picture. It's different for everyone, but for me at least, God answers me with a lot of questions and cryptic statements (i.e. you already know the answer).

Regardless of how unhelpful that may seem, I actually DO find it helpful to clarify my thoughts. (And, again, yours may look totally different than mine.)

Once you've gotten clear around what beliefs you're going to shift and what action you're going to take to shift them, it's just a matter of following your Money and Mindset Breakthrough Plan. (And remember, you're never going to actually be "done" here. Every time you grow and move to the next level, your "stuff" is going to pop up and try and trip you up again, which is why having a daily practice can help ground you and keep you connected to your Source and Inner Wisdom, so you don't let life derail you.)

Also, it's important to keep in mind that I don't necessarily expect you to have your Money and Mindset Breakthrough Plan filled out completely right now. There are still a lot more exercises and topics to cover, but this gets you started so you can begin shifting your beliefs right now. Then, you can simply add to your plan as you discover new exercises you want to try.

Chapter 6
WHAT ABOUT ALL THOSE VOICES IN YOUR HEAD?

An amazing thing happens as you begin integrating fear-based emotions: the noise in your head gets a lot quieter.

At least it did for me.

In retrospect, I think what was happening was when I would start to feel a fear-based emotion, my way of burying or running from that emotion was to start worrying about it, so I had this constant cacophony of different voices talking (and even arguing with one another) in my head.

That made it virtually impossible to hear the soft, gentle voice of my intuition/inner wisdom, or feel the pull of my desire.

Here's another way to look at this. Dan is highly-intuitive, and feels his truth in his gut. When he is "in his head," thinking about the future, it creates a lot of anxiety in him, which manifests as a knot in his gut. The knot is overwhelming, which results in keeping him from accessing his intuitive side. But when he focuses on breathing deeply, into his belly, he is able to relax, get out of his head, and into his body, so he can then trust what his gut wants to tell him.

When you can't hear or feel your intuition/inner wisdom or feel the pull of your desire, it's very difficult to keep from relying on other people and outside influences for guidance. And, once you start listening to other people over what you know deep down to be true for you, that's when you wake up one day wondering how on earth you ended up living someone else's life.

It's a bit of a cycle:

The more you start listening to your intuition, the less you'll be controlled by your inner critics and the easier it will be to do what needs to be done to move yourself toward the life of your dreams. On the flip side, the more you allow your inner critic to dictate your actions, the less you'll be able to hear your intuition (or the less you'll trust what you hear), and the unhappier you'll likely be with your life.

So, this chapter is designed to help you strengthen your relationship with your intuition or inner wisdom, and stop letting your inner critics (or inner mean girls/dudes) run the show.

But to better understand the relationship between your inner critic and your intuition, let's start by looking more closely at your desires.

Eva Gregory says if you have a desire for something, not only is it real, but it's something you should be actively pursuing. We don't have desires for things that are not ours to obtain. But if we're resisting our desire in some way (like with mindset blocks, or energetically, or when we are not in alignment) then metaphorically, our hands are closed into fists: the Universe can't deliver what we desire, even if it's trying to. Nor can you accept it with a closed fist, which is what happens when you are not open to receiving.

But the moment you relax your "hand," the Universe can deliver it to you.

Let me give you an example. Let's say you want money, and you're working desperately hard to get money, but money isn't flowing to you.

In this case, what's probably going on is you're resisting money in some way, so once you give up resisting, money will flow.

So the obvious question becomes, HOW do you stop resisting?

You raise your vibration, so you're energetically aligned with making money (which I'm covering in the next chapter), and you work on your mindset blocks around money so you won't fall into a story trap like, "Well, I guess money isn't going to flow to me," or, "I guess God doesn't want me to have money." (As Eva says, it's not God; it's your gremlins keeping it from you.) As much as possible, you also want to stay focused on the outcome you want to create.

Keep in mind you're always doing one of two things here: either energizing the fear that you haven't manifested your desire, or energizing the emotion around the solution.

Our mind chatter often tends to inadvertently "mix up" our focus, by including both aspects of what we want and don't want, making it difficult to receive what we actually DO want. (Yup – you got it – total confusion!).

Following are some examples, from Pamelah Landers of what this looks like:

"I need more money because I don't have enough." In this case, your vibration is not receiving. Rather, it's focused on the lack perspective.

As opposed to:

"I feel good when money flows to me, and I'm open to receiving it in ways I may not be aware of." This is a solution-focused, receiving vibration."I need to generate income. If I don't have enough by the 1st, I won't be able to pay rent." Again, this is not a receiving vibration. It's actually problem-focused.

As opposed to: "My intuition knows there is a solution for this, and my next step is to connect with my inner guidance/inner knowing/God/Angels/Divine/Source, and ask for clarity while being open to receiving it." Again, this is a solution-focused, receiving vibration.

The more you can focus on the solution, the easier and faster you'll be able to manifest it.

Now, just because you stop resisting your desires doesn't mean you stop working. You definitely need to take action. But rather than forcing things or trying to make things happen through sheer willpower, you allow the Universe (or God) to help you out. (I'll talk more about surrendering and letting God/Universe help you in the next chapter.)

Also, keep in mind that how your desire actually manifests itself may not always LOOK how you think it ought to look, or how you expected it to - which is why *being committed to your desire but not attached to how it actually unfolds* is key to this process.

I'm also a big believer that for the most part, it's never too late to achieve your desires. Now, if you have a desire to win an Olympic gold medal and you're fifty years old, that may no longer be possible. But, who's to say you wouldn't be able to coach an Olympic gold medalist - or be a part of that dream another way? (Remember, stay committed but not attached.)

Which leads me to one of the reasons we tend to resist our desires: we listen to those awful negative voices chattering away in our head.

My good friends Christine Arylo and Amy Ahlers, best-selling authors and co-creators of *Reform Your Inner Mean Girl* (which has helped over 30,000 women worldwide to shift their self-sabotaging patterns and mindsets into self-empowering and supportive habits and actions), call these voices the Inner Mean Girls (or Inner Mean Dudes), and they've created an entire system around Reforming Your Inner Mean Girl. (They also have a book you can check out.)

Now, I know it seems simple. Inner mean girls? Just dump them. Right? And all your problems with resistance will be solved.

Well, not so much.

As much as you may want to send your Inner Mean Girls packing, that's not how it works. (Quite honestly, that strategy doesn't work for *any* shadow work. The more you try to hide or squelch your shadow or the things you don't like about yourself, the more you'll find yourself controlled by them.)

Believe it or not, your Inner Mean Girls were actually created to help you. Yes, they've gotten a bit twisted somewhere along the way and have since turned into a hindrance rather than a help, but I promise you, their original role was to keep you safe. (Remember what we covered earlier, about core wounds. Your Inner Mean Girls help you survive and cope. Embracing them could have a huge benefit.)

The problem is, keeping you safe is not the same thing as making you happy. In fact, I would go as far to say in many cases, keeping you safe and making you happy are actually opposites of each other.

There's safety in the familiar (or at least the illusion of safety), even if the familiar isn't what you actually want and is, in reality, making you very unhappy. Not taking chances or risks is safe, because if you take a chance and it doesn't work out, then you could end up in a worse situation than you are in right now.

For example, you could feel familiar and safe in your one bedroom apartment in which you have lived for five years. You may not be happy with the location, because it's too noisy, or the neighbors because they are inconsiderate about noise. But you tolerate these things because moving doesn't feel safe, or it's too much work, or too hard to find a new place for such a great price, etc. What if moving to a new town or taking a job in another location required you to move? Would you be open to that, knowing that more happiness was in fact available?

How can you actually go after your dreams or your desires if you don't take any chances?

Now, just because your Inner Mean Girl's original intent was to help you doesn't mean you need to keep her around. What Amy and Christine teach is a process to help you first identify your Inner Mean Girl or Girls (yes, it's very common to have multiple Inner Mean Girls), and then assure them they don't need to keep you safe anymore - you've got that covered. Then, you give them a new job that actually will help you rather than hinder you.

For me, my Inner Mean Girls never really took to their new jobs very well and kept sliding back into being, well, mean. (However, remember what I shared about core wounds; just because something doesn't work exactly right for me doesn't mean it won't work differently for you.)

Regardless of what my Inner Mean Girls did in my situation, I found this work invaluable. Taking the time to identify them has allowed me to recognize them when they decide to pipe in - which has consequently allowed me to recognize them quickly, stop listening to them, and better identify the voice of my intuition, or what Christine and Amy call my Inner Wisdom.

Now, being able to hear the voice of your intuition or Inner Wisdom is only half the battle - you also need to be able to *trust that what you're receiving is indeed your intuition*.

Pamelah Landers is one expert who (among other things) helps teach folks how to tune into and trust their intuition. It's incredibly important, because if you're not tuning in to it, or not trusting what you receive, then you're also not going to take action. (And, of course, if you have mindset blocks in the way, even if you tune into and trust your intuition, your blocks will keep you from taking action.)

She says there are a lot of ways your intuition can communicate with you - your job is to recognize when it is communicating, and to continuously practice trusting it (which will in turn help strengthen it). In other words, learning to trust your intuitive insights allows you to receive more of them. Your intuition is always available to you.

You may receive intuitive insights in one or more of the following ways:

1. You hear words or voices.

2. You see visions, pictures, images or symbols.

3. Your body feels the "truth" of something – you may get chills or tingles, for example.

4. You just "KNOW" something is true or accurate intuitively, or you know it isn't – this is a "cognitive knowing."

5. You FEEL empathy in your body. You feel somebody else's feelings, and experience "intuitive knowing."

6. You have insights, learning, experiences, and/or desires in dreams.

Pamelah's intuition communicates with her primarily through words and voices. She often receives "one liners" from guidance, like, "You will be moving out of this space between November and January." Secondarily, Pamelah also sees visions and images, and sometimes, she just "knows" something is accurate or true because her entire body feels completely aligned. An example is knowing when somebody is aligned with what they are saying and it's actually true for them, or when they are "in their head," making it up.

It's also important to know the difference between ego/mind chatter (or your Inner Mean Girls or Dudes) and your intuition. One good way to identify what you're receiving is to pay attention to how the information FEELS: your intuition tends to feel clear and is always for your highest good. Your ego/mind chatter tends to feel muddled or limiting, is often negative, and not for your highest good.

Also, for myself, my intuition will answer me, but will only answer me once. It doesn't repeat itself. Whereas my mind chatter and Inner Mean Girls will repeat themselves and frankly never shut up about the point they're trying to make.

There may be some times when you're totally unclear about what your intuition is trying to tell you. In that case, you may need to talk with other people to access it. Someone else may have the answer you're seeking. Remember, everyone is intuitive and everyone has different gifts. Seeking support is natural. Asking for help is strength.

Pamelah also observes that people's intuitive skill sets are not all the same, not only in relation to the styles listed above, but also in regard to what they have access to receive. For example, some people can see visions about where another person's best path will take them, while others may be more intuitive around current emotions, feelings, and truth telling, while being not at all connected with the future. Knowing what your areas of expertise are around your intuition, and not comparing those areas to others, will further support your choices.

Now that we've covered what's going on with your brain when you're resisting, and how your mind could be stopping you, let's shift to some other factors that might also be contributing to your resistance – namely, the energy and vibration of money.

Chapter 7
RAISING YOUR VIBRATION

Everything is energy.

In physics class, we learned that if you shrink everything down to molecules, those molecules are vibrating with energy.

Our personal energy is what fuels our life and business. When we take action, we need energy to do it, and taking action releases energy.

Even our thoughts and emotions are energy. (Note: Did you know our emotions have a distinct smell to them as well, which is why our dogs can actually smell if we're happy, sad, angry, etc.? Or have you ever been in a room and "sensed" someone was sad or angry? You may not have known what the problem was, but you knew something was going on. Do you know people who drain you? On the flip side, have you known people who are so happy and full of joy it's contagious, and you feel so much better when you're in their presence? My point here is that emotions are REAL, and as I mentioned earlier, they can get trapped in our bodies. Too often, we're led to believe that they're just "in our heads" … but that is not the case.)

It was said that Mother Theresa could be a block away from the worst parts of Calcutta, and people would start to calm down and relax. That's how powerful her energy was.

We are all literally vibrating with energy. And, as we also learned in physics, energy attracts like energy.

So, if we're vibrating at a "low" frequency, we "attract" a lot of negativity and problems, more so than if we're vibrating at a higher frequency.

Now, this doesn't mean if we raise our vibration, we'll never have a bad day. What it means is if we raise our vibration, we'll attract more people, opportunities, and experiences that align with that vibration.

Your vibration will not always be high or always be low. Our vibration fluctuates, depending on what's going on in our lives. (This is also why the expression "bad things come in threes" exists. Often, when something happens to put us in a bad mood, our vibration lowers and then suddenly, we're practically a magnet for all sorts of crappy things. And yes, it works in reverse as well: if our vibration is high, we'll attract good things in groups too.)

So the bottom line here is this:

If we're looking to attract more money into our lives, raising our vibration is an excellent way to do it.

Let me illustrate with a story.

Let's say you're really scared and worried right now, because cash flow is low and you're not sure how you're going to pay next month's bills.

But you have a sales call with a potential client that could change everything.

If you get on that call with that potential client full of fear and desperation (let's be honest: if you really, really need to close the sale, it's desperation, right?), how do you think you're going to come across to that prospect? Needy? Pushy? In full pursuit mode?

Desperate. That's exactly how you'll come across.

And, chances are, that prospect won't move forward with you, because she doesn't want to be around that kind of energy, or if she does say "yes," she will be the wrong client for you.

But if you're able to shift your vibration so you're relaxed and not attached to closing that sale, the whole conversation will shift, and so will your energy (think confidence instead of desperation). Then, the prospect will be more likely to move forward with you.

Which brings me to how to raise your vibration, and the two paths toward doing so.

The long-term path is the one you're on right now, reading this book. Over time, you move through your subconscious and mindset blocks and integrate your fear-based emotions to raise your vibration.

The short-term path is the one you take when you're having a bad day, and you want to shift your energy to stop attracting more negative circumstances. Or, maybe you want to raise your vibration before a sales call.

Now, your feelings play a BIG part in the energy you're projecting, so the more you get a handle on your emotions, the higher your vibration will become.

Let's dig into some "in the moment" exercises now (which also will help raise your vibration overall if you do it every day, so you can use these exercises for both the long and short-term paths).

EXERCISE: Gratitude

Gratitude is one of the highest forms of vibration. Therefore, if your vibration is really low, doing gratitude exercises is one of the best ways to start to raise it.

Elizabeth Purvis has a great gratitude exercise I'm going to share with you, but first, I want to share her story.

In 2010, Elizabeth was still pretty new in her business. She was getting ready to launch her signature program for the first time. Now, if you're an entrepreneur, you probably know that launching a product or program can generate enough stress and anxiety to lower your vibration. In Elizabeth's case, she was also "coming out of the closet," so to speak.

She was launching her Goddess Business School, which was all about bringing the Divine Feminine into business. At the time, this was a big deal because unlike now, where there seems to be a new mystery school or feminine business school popping up every week, back then, it wasn't really talked about.

She had no idea how her school would land with the marketplace. She didn't know if she was going to hurt her reputation, if anyone would hire her after revealing her passion, etc. Plus, she really didn't want to be identified as a healer, which is where this new direction was heading.

And, as icing on the cake, things hadn't been great for Elizabeth financially, so she was feeling an incredible amount of pressure to have that particular launch be successful.

In other words, she was pretty stressed.

Now, she knew that if she allowed her stress and mind chatter to overwhelm her (which she was definitely in danger of doing), she would never get herself in the right emotional state to write her email copy, market her launch or attract the money she needed to reach her financial goals.

So, she instituted a gratitude practice.

Elizabeth chose to do it first thing in the morning, before she even got out of bed. She found if she allowed her day and to-dos to start creeping into her brain, she would be too distracted and overwhelmed to quiet her mind enough to focus on gratitude, so it was important for her to do it right away. (While you can practice gratitude anytime, first thing in the morning or last thing before you go to bed are two of the most powerful times to do it.)

So every morning, Elizabeth would focus on three things she was grateful for. And they weren't always big and earth-shattering. Sometimes she was grateful to have a roof over her head, her husband sleeping beside her, and a working computer with high-speed internet.

The thing is, you can ALWAYS find things to be grateful for.

Even if you feel like your life is utter crap right now, there IS something to be grateful for. You have food in your fridge, you're about to make yourself a cup of coffee, you have clothes in your closet, you have heat, you have running water (you see where I'm going with this). There are plenty of people in this world who do not have those basic necessities, so it's good to remember you really DO have a lot to be grateful for.

For Elizabeth, her gratitude practice worked, and she was able to shift her mindset and ultimately manifest $50,000.

EXERCISE: Mindfulness Bell

I covered this tool in Chapter Five, but it's worth mentioning again here because whereas before I covered how to use the Mindfulness Bell to interrupt patterns, you can also use it to raise your vibration.

So as a quick reminder, this tool and exercise comes from my friend Eva Gregory. The Mindfulness Bell is actually an app you can download (there are both free and paid versions).

Remember, you can set it so a bell goes off randomly throughout your day or at specific times (maybe once an hour). When the bell goes off, that's your cue to stop what you're doing and check in with how you're feeling.

Are you feeling a little frantic? Overwhelmed? Angry? Frustrated?

If you're feeling an uncomfortable, fear-based emotion and would rather feel at peace, take a few minutes to close your eyes, breathe and *BE in the present moment.*

Yesterday is gone, and the future is not promised. All you have is the present.

So re-center. Focus on the present moment.

Feel and breathe into whatever emotion you're feeling, and you'll start to shift that emotion so you can release it.

Now, while you don't necessarily need an app or a bell to remind you to stop, breathe and be present with your emotions, the problem is when you DO start spinning around in an uncomfortable emotion - like overwhelm or frustration or anger - it's difficult to realize you ARE spinning around. It's hard to see that you are trapped in the emotions of the moment. Having something exterior interrupt whatever craziness you're trapped inside of can be extremely effective.

Another variation of using the Mindfulness Bell is learning how to surrender when everything starts to pile up.

For example, let's say you're in the middle of a big deadline for a client and your computer crashes. You summon technical help, which turns out to be not-so-helpful, and you aren't able to get your computer back up and running.

Now, in this exact moment, you may be feeling out-of-control. You may want to blame someone – anyone! - and point fingers at something so you can hold someone or something responsible for the chaos that's happening.

The problem is, if we do act on those feelings and throw a fit (maybe yell at our technical support team) then we're acting on (or reacting to) that energy's vibration.

If, however, we instead choose to surrender to the moment, to what's happening, and breathe into those feelings without acting on them, chances are a solution will end up revealing itself.

Now, a lot of people misunderstand the use of the word "surrender." They think what that really means is we're giving up, which is not at all true.

Surrender is about allowing God/Source in to help. Surrender is about not having to do everything yourself, struggling to use sheer willpower or force to make things stop, or happen. Surrender is allowing help to rush in when we need it most.

Surrender is to "Let Go and Let God."

(Note: the first time I heard the phrase "Let Go and Let God," I was completely confused. It made absolutely no sense to me. Then I spent a week in the ICU with my extremely sick mother, who I thought was dying. I remember being left alone on what I thought was going to be her last day. She couldn't talk because she had a breathing tube, and the room was silent except for the quiet murmur of the machines. I was holding her hand, crying and trying to read to her. I had two thoughts running simultaneously through my head over and over: "I'm not going to die with my books inside me," and "Let Go and Let God."

The second one was important because there was nothing the doctors could do for her - they made that very clear - and they fully expected her not to make it. So, there was really nothing to do: nothing for me to solve, nothing for me to force or figure out, nothing to research. And as someone who lives in her brain, whose business is based on mentally solving my clients' problems, this was WAY out of my comfort zone. I couldn't heal my mother using my mind. The only thing I could do was be with her, hold her hand, and do my best to read to her. And that's when I finally "got" the God phrase, at a deep level. In something of a miracle, the next day my mother made a sudden recovery and lived for about nine more months. The doctors were stunned by the turn of the events. Now, I'm not going to promise chanting the phrase "Let Go and Let God" over and over will result in the same miracle I experienced, but the point is, surrendering works. When everything else feels out of your control, try it. Give in. Let Go, and Let God.

EXERCISE: I Brag

Melinda Cohan shared this tool with me - it's specifically for women, since men generally already know how to brag. ☺

(That said, clearly if you're a man who has trouble bragging, feel free to use this exercise too.)

First, let me define "bragging" as I'm using it here: I'm not talking about being arrogant or rude or putting other people down. I'm talking about taking a moment to acknowledge what's good in your life.

Women are taught to be nice, quiet and polite. We learn that it's acceptable to shine a big, bright light on other people's accomplishments, but not on our own.

I Brag allows you to acknowledge your truth and speak it with your voice, and because you acknowledge it, you activate more of it. Bragging also strengthens our ability to own our "power muscle."

And, even more importantly, bragging allows us to acknowledge what's good in our lives, because unacknowledged good turns to crap.

It's like a Thanksgiving meal - you've eaten all this wonderful food and are completely stuffed, and if you don't take the time to digest what you've eaten before eating more, you're going to make yourself really sick.

Bragging is the way to digest the good things that happen to you.

So, it works like this:

You begin by saying: "I have the most amazing brag," and then you say your brag.

You can do this to start an email, at the start of a meeting, or even the start of a conversation.

There's also a Part Two to this particular exercise, which is called "the up-ride."

Whoever is hearing/reading the brag does the up-ride, which sounds like this:

"I want to up-ride you and share one of the things I find amazing about you ..."

This is a deeper acknowledgement of the positive, AND it comes from a community member, which is important to us as women since we are community-oriented. (Back in hunter/gatherer days, women lived and raised children together in a community, and needed a community to physically survive. This is why it's deeply embedded in us to be a part of a community.)

The up-ride also acts as a witnessing to the brag, and allows the person doing the brag to sit in a space and receive - which again, as women, gives us the chance to allow ourselves to receive compliments (something else we don't do nearly as often as we should).

You can also expand on the I Brag tool and turn it into a Trinity. You start with a brag, follow up with gratitude, and then end with desire.

It looks like this:

- ♥ "I have the most amazing brag ..."

- ♥ "I'm grateful for ..."

- ♥ "I desire ..."

Once the trinity is complete, the up-ride of the brag occurs.

And then, the other person answers, "And so it shall be, beyond your wildest dreams."

The desire part is pretty cool, because after your brag and practicing of gratitude, you'll have raised your vibration, so it will be the perfect time to put your desire out there so the Universe can co-create it with you. It's important to be as clear as you can be with your desire: the clearer you are, the more likely you are to receive it.

Now that we've covered the mindset piece, it's time to move into what you've probably been waiting for: the "Show Me the Money!" piece.

Ready?

Let's dig into money-attraction strategies.

Part 3

STRATEGIES TO ATTRACT MONEY AND WEALTH

Chapter 8
YOUR MONEY FOUNDATION

So It's my belief that money is one of the most misunderstood things out there.

That's why we tend to have such a complicated relationship with it.

On the surface, it seems pretty simple. Money is just the paper or coin we use to purchase things, and we can pretty much buy anything we desire … from products to people's time to their expertise and more.

So, how does something so simple end up being so complicated?

It's because of what money *represents* to us, and the emotions we have around those representations.

To some, money means security. It means having the ability to provide for your family the way you want.

It can represent freedom, since it is a means having the ability to do the things you love, like traveling.

It can also be the means to owning status symbols, like expensive cars and houses.

It can enable you to give back … to make an impact.

And it can also trigger emotions - many of them fear-based.

As Kendra E Thornbury points out, money is fundamental to our survival, so there is survival energy around it. And when you're in a space of survival, you limit your ability to be creative, innovative, and productive. If it gets bad enough - for instance, if you're faced with losing your home because you can't pay your mortgage or rent - it can trigger a fight-or-flight response. And when you're in survival or fight/flight mode, you're operating at a very low vibration while limiting your ability to access higher thought processes in your brain (which can perpetuate the cycle).

Money is complicated.

We may feel shame or guilt or anger or resentment or unworthiness (or a combination of these emotions) when we think about money.

We may feel like if we love what we do, we shouldn't charge for it (or charge much for it).

We may feel if we're spiritual/heart-based, we shouldn't charge for what we do.

We may feel like we don't offer enough value to charge what we really want to charge.

We may feel like we need to read more books or get more certifications or finish college before we can actually charge what we want to for our time.

We may worry if we make more money than our spouse or parents or friends, they'll no longer love us and will leave us.

We may feel rich people are greedy SOBs - which means we'll never be rich because we don't want to turn into a greedy SOB too.

And, even if we're making good money - maybe we're even making a lot of money - we still can be consumed by it, because then we are living in fear around losing what we have. So we remain focused on making more, and are continuously stressed when we don't hit those higher financial goals.

Examining our relationship with money in order to attract more of it is one of the biggest reasons the entrepreneurship journey is also a personal development journey.

Money is tied to so many things in our life. That's why, the more we can acknowledge and integrate the shadow side of money, the more we can move toward having an abundant, healthy relationship with money.

The best way to start creating that abundant, healthy relationship is to look closely at what's holding you back from it.

Let's start with an exercise to start uncovering the negative thoughts and feelings that may be at the root of your money challenges.

EXERCISE: The Root Cause of Your Money Challenges

This is a journaling exercise, so get out that paper and pen again.

Take a few moments to think about - and answer - the following questions:

1. How do I feel about money?

2. How do I feel about rich people, or those who make a lot of money?

3. How do I feel when I think about asking for money for a service or product I'm offering in my business?

4. If you're offering a service (or thinking of offering a service), write down the hourly rate you're considering charging. Now put a zero at the end of it. Then answer this: How does that make me feel? (Write down everything that comes up for you.)

5. How do I feel about the amount of money I'm making now?

6. How would I feel if I started making over $100,000 a year? Over $500,000? Over a million dollars? What comes up for me?

7. How would I feel if my income was suddenly cut in half?

Don't overthink; just write. And write down EVERYTHING you can think of. Especially focus on all the fears you may have about making more money, or not having enough.

What you really want to get at are your beliefs about money that are holding you back.

For instance, your answers might sound like this:

- ✓ I don't deserve to make a lot of money.

- ✓ Who am I to charge so much?

- ✓ There's never enough; I need to make more.

- ✓ Once I start making X amount, I'll feel happy and peaceful.

- ✓ I'm spiritual; I shouldn't charge for what I do.

- ✓ I love what I do; I shouldn't charge for it.

✔ I want to change the world/make a difference/heal people. I shouldn't charge for it. That makes me selfish.

✔ I can't make more money than my parents/spouse/ friends. They may stop loving me and/or leave me if I do.

✔ Rich people are greedy and selfish.

✔ My biggest fear is ending up a bag lady sleeping under a bridge.

✔ I'm unlucky with money.

✔ It's the economy's fault that I can't make more money.

You get the idea.

Once you get them all out, take a look at what you've written. Chances are you'll see a common theme start to emerge.

You may also want to take a moment and group each of your answers under one of the following categories:

💜 Money as related to your value/worth (i.e. "Who am I to charge this much?")

💜 Money as related to family/community/love (i.e. "Will my family stop loving me/leave me if I make more money?")

- Money as a victim consciousness (i.e. blaming the economy, your luck or someone or something else for your money woes)

- Money and culture (i.e. "Rich people are evil.")

- Money and "enough-ness" (i.e. anything around feeling like you need to make more because there's not enough, or your fears about ending up a bag lady)

Now, don't panic if you discover you have a lot of money blocks, and they span multiple categories. Again, our relationship with money is complicated. It's not uncommon to have several money-related blocks.

So, one of the first things I would encourage you to do is start to integrate and work through those blocks, and the best way to start that work is to go back to Chapter Three and go through the exercises for each of the beliefs or blocks you've just identified.

This alone has the power to shift your finances in a positive way. Plus, the more you work through your blocks, the faster all the other money-attraction exercises will start working for you.

I also want to encourage you to look at something called your "money set point," or your "having level," as both of these contribute to your current financial situation.

Your Money Set Point/Having Level

Your money set point is the amount of money your subconscious has decided is "safe" for you to make. So, if your money set point if $50,000, that's how much you make.

The good news is it's difficult for you to make less than your money set point. So, let's say you end up getting sick and can't generate income for a few months. You'll probably find the money "magically" coming in faster than normal to make up for the months you don't work.

The bad news is that it's also difficult to make more than your set point. So, in this case, once you've gotten "caught up," the money flow will probably slow down. Or, if you get an unexpected windfall - maybe an unexpected check of $10,000 shows up over and above your money set point - the next day your car breaks down and your roof starts leaking, and suddenly that "windfall" disappears in unexpected bills.

To figure out your set point, take a look at about how much money you've been generating over the past few years. Whatever the average is, that's likely your set point.

Your "having level" is from the book *The Big Leap*, and it's a similar concept to the set point. The way Hendricks describes it, your brain only allows you to have so much love or money or happiness before it sabotages you.[7]

So, for instance, let's say you have a wonderful night with your spouse; you really connect on a deep level. And then, the next

7   *The Big Leap*

morning, your spouse does that thing again that irritates you so much, you say something, and the next thing you know, you're smack dab in the middle of a huge fight.

That happens because you went above your "having level" for love and happiness, so to "even you out," your subconscious started a fight.

In both cases, it's entirely possible to reset your set point and increase your "having level." You just have to do it consciously. In the case of your set point, working on whatever blocks or beliefs that have gotten you stuck at your current financial set point is the first step. (And to do that, go back through your list of money beliefs and then work though each of them with the exercises in Chapter Three.) And then, to expand beyond that growth, use meditations and affirmations. (I'll be covering affirmations in more detail in Chapter 12.)

Okay, so now that we've covered the money beliefs that are holding you back, let's start looking at some new definitions of money that encourage it to flow into your life.

Chapter 10
OLD VERSUS NEW MONEY BELIEFS

In the book *The Soul of Money*, Lynn Twist talks about the toxic myths related to scarcity, including "there's never enough" and "more is better."[8]

Basically, these myths fall under the fear "umbrella" that we are not enough, or we don't have enough, which then drives an unhealthy focus on making money above everything else.

When you combine this with all the other issues around money - our fears around how having more money would fundamentally hurt our relationship with ourselves and/or our loved ones, or how it brings out our victim consciousness - it's no wonder so many of us have money challenges.

But, it really doesn't have to be this way.

We can choose to view all the beliefs that are blocking our money flow as old beliefs, and replace them with new, healthy, empowering beliefs.

To help you do that, I've included a list of different ideas and new beliefs around money. None are necessarily right or wrong. If you don't resonate with any of them, don't use them. But, my hope is that just the act of reading them may open something up in you.

---

8   Lynn Twist, *The Soul of Money* (2006)

Just because you've always believed in those old money beliefs doesn't mean they're true, or that you necessarily need to keep believing them.

So, here's some new perspective!

Money as an exchange of energy.

Like everything else, money is energy. And when you purchase something, you're simply exchanging energy.

Whatever it is you're purchasing has energy in it: the energy it took to create it. And, when you exchange the energy of money for the energy of what you're purchasing, you've now balanced both sides of the ledger, and (if it's a fair exchange), you both feel complete.

This might help all of you who feel like you shouldn't charge because you're spiritual, or because you're trying to make a difference in the world, or because you really love what you do.

If you aren't valuing what you've spent your energy creating (if you don't charge for it, you've put no value on it), you've created an imbalance. Your clients will feel like they "owe" you, and that's an uncomfortable feeling.

By putting a price tag on what you're creating with your energy, you're actually giving people a way to *honor your energy* by exchanging it with the energy of money.

Money as an exchange of value.

This is a pretty common way to view money - as an exchange of value. You have something of value and you're exchanging it for something else of value. The more valuable your offering, the more money you can charge for it.

Spiritual Misunderstandings about Money:

Mellissa Seaman, Stanford-educated former attorney turned Intuitive Business Strategist, has an interesting take on this. First off, she says you do need to come to peace with money being the global measure of value - even if you're bartering, and even if you're a spiritual person who resents money's existence, you still need some sort of surrendering to the concept that money is a measurement of value.

However, she really hates the whole "charge what you're worth" phrasing. You are invaluable. You can't put a price on yourself. You also can't charge anything you want for your services, because obviously, people will only pay what they are willing to invest in the moment for the value of your services.

People pay for what you are promising. So what is the value of the benefits you're promising? That's what you should charge.

Money as a thank you.

Mellissa calls money a "thank you."

142

She invites us to think of money as a gift.

Clients are thanking her when they pay her. In addition to delivering on the promised benefits of the work, they are paying her for the intangible benefits she provides in a session: hope, motivation, and the support of a trustworthy ally.

Money as a sacred ritual.

When money is given in trust, Mellissa says, it's a deep covenant. It's a sacrifice. Just like in a sacred ritual, money can represent intention, investment, and the kind of sacrifice that brings magic.

In fact, when a client pays her four or five figures, Mellissa performs a short, informal ritual with the client the moment his or her credit card is charged. Her clients are sacrificing their money to get the results they're looking for in their life, and as they're sacrificing serious money, she honors the magic of the moment. She takes a few minutes to acknowledge the sacrifice and to invoke support from higher realms to assist the sacred covenant of service they are creating together.

Honoring the sacred moment of payment gives dignity, depth, and power to a moment that is too often brushed over in a busy life and practice. It also honors the fear and risk that people face when they invest significant amounts in themselves. It honors the leap of faith they are making. It lets them know that you take it seriously, too. It puts the fear of the expenditure to work as a sacrifice that can bring major benefits in the magic of faith and commitment.

Money is fun/a hoot.

This one (and the next) is from Suzy Prudden, Internationally Acclaimed Speaker, Workshop and Seminar Leader, and New York Times Best Selling Author (from before the internet) who we'll be hearing more from in later chapters.

What if you truly believed money is fun? What would change in your life?

Let that sink in for a minute.

If you want to do a lot of good, then you want a lot of money.

Suzy's grandfather was very wealthy, and he spent his money being a philanthropist. He bought people's freedom from concentration camps. Yet, when he traveled, he would travel third class. If you asked him why he traveled third class, he would tell you, "Because there's no fourth class."

If you want to do a lot of good and you don't have a lot of money, all you have to trade for doing a lot of good is your time, which is wonderful and noble … and limiting.

There's only so much good you're going to be able to do if all you can do is volunteer your time.

But, instead, consider what you could accomplish and how much good you could do if you had a lot of money.

Money *wants* to love you.

This is from a few different experts, and we're going to dig more into this one in the next chapter, so watch for that. Yes, it's a bit woo-woo and yes, it also has the power to rock your world.

Money is sacred.

Kendra E Thornbury teaches that not only is it possible to love money, but loving money can actually be part of your spiritual practice.

Kendra has an amazing money story. She started her business and moved into a cottage on ten acres of land. At that time, she was also struggling with money. Her business was new and not generating much income: she had exhausted her resources, maxed out her credit cards, borrowed as much as she could from her family, and even sold her car.

She felt scared all the time. She would stay up all night worrying about paying the rent.

Finally, one day she realized she couldn't live in that chronic state of stress any longer. She had had enough.

She had no Plan B, and she wasn't getting a j-o-b, so she knew she had to make her business work. So, she took a good, long look at how she viewed money.

What she found was that she did in fact have limiting beliefs around money. She viewed it as bad, evil ... she believed it was the reason we are screwed up as a society, etc.

Once she realized she had these limiting beliefs, she wondered what might happen if she turned them around, and decided to love money instead. What if she could take that even further, and make loving money part of her spiritual practice?

She shifted her beliefs so that money became sacred. She worked on believing that money is energy; money is a loving source that wants to provide for her. She meditated on it, she got down on her knees and declared that to the Universe, and guess what? Her finances started to shift for the better.

Kendra is now fierce about taking a stand to shift your money foundation to one of love instead of fear. She feels that too many people allow money to bring out their victim consciousness. While there is no question money can make you feel like a victim - I know for years I felt like money's "plaything" and had no say in when money would show up and when it wouldn't - you can shift your thinking to get rid of this block.

146

And by the way, the worst part of being in victim mode around money is it perpetrates your money problems. Ugh!

Money is neutral.

This comes from Kendra as well - money is just a *thing*. It's neutral.

We're the ones who attach the meaning to it, and we're the ones who set up and maintain a system that perpetuates money issues.

Don't buy into the idea that you need to be financially broke to be spiritually rich. Quite honestly, there's no way you can run a successful business and show up powerfully for your clients if you're worried about money. It's like when you're on an airplane and they tell you to put your oxygen mask on before helping others - you can't help anyone if you're passed out in your seat. And you certainly can't help your clients if you're consumed with worry about paying your bills.

You are enough/There is enough.

In the book *The Soul of Money*, Lynn Twist talks about how there truly is enough, and once you believe that, you'll be "in the flow" of abundance.[9]

Nature operates under this same principle. No more, no less. And, it's possible for us to live our lives believing the same.

---

9   *The Soul of Money*

Now, this doesn't mean we shouldn't have savings and practice good financial management. That's just being smart with our money. But, what it does mean is there's no need to hoard money, or to worry about running out.

Money is money - not to be confused with other emotional needs.

Mellissa Seaman shared that one of the biggest mistakes you can make when it comes to placing value is confusing one value with another. So, for instance, what you may be craving is love, connection, and being on purpose, but instead, you end up focusing on making more money.

We think we're buying those things with money, but alas … those are actually the things we lose.

Kendra also talked about this: the dangers of using money to fulfill an emotional need it can't solve. Back when she lived in the cottage and was at the height of her money struggles, she started to realize she was trying to use money to fulfill an emotional need it had no business filling.

Once she identified the emotional need, she started looking at other ways to serve it.

Some things she ended up doing included:

💜 Meditating consistently

- Connecting with Source

- Structuring her financial house

- Creating better habits around food to help her feel more nourished

- Looking inside herself for the answers

EXERCISE: Money Versus Emotional Needs

You too may have confused making money with a different emotional need, like one of those listed above.

To help you sort that out, Kendra recommends asking yourself:

- ✔ What does money represent to me?

- ✔ What is the emotional need I think money will fulfill for me?

Really take some time to digest all of this, and to write down your answers. You may also want to do some journaling around these questions as well.

Once you've gotten some clarity around what your emotional need is, the next step is to create a daily practice designed to fulfill that emotional need for you.

Along with what Kendra did herself, you could also do things like carve out time to do things that make you feel loved and pampered, like taking long hot baths or exercising. Or, maybe you need to spend more time with your family or friends. There's no wrong answer: do whatever helps you serve that emotional need.

Chapter 10
YOURE RELATIONSHIP WITH MONEY

In my research, I've discovered that money-attraction strategies tend to fall under one of two camps - the practical and the "woo-woo."

I'm covering strategies from both in this book.

Fair warning:

In this chapter, we are definitely traveling down the woo-woo path.

However, before we get too deeply into the woo-woo, let's start by explaining what I mean when I say "your relationship with money."

So, first off, you have one. A relationship, that is.

It doesn't matter how practical you are or how solid your feet are planted on the ground - everyone has a relationship with money.

Yes, yes ... I know money isn't something that's actually alive, so the idea of having a relationship with a nonliving thing can feel sort of weird. Nonetheless, it doesn't change the fact that you DO have a relationship with it.

Let me give you some examples of what your money relationship may feel like:

- There's never enough. It doesn't matter how hard you work or what you do, at the end of day, you have more bills than money to pay them. **Maybe you feel like money is never there for you.**

- You have no trouble generating a lot of money … but keeping it is another story. As easily as it flows to you, it flows right back out the door in a never-ending cycle of expenses and bills. **Maybe you feel like your relationship with money is fleeting - here today, gone tomorrow.**

- You're paying your bills, but no matter what you do, you can't seem to get ahead. A big bonus comes in, a new client, a raise - it's fabulous, and you celebrate. And then, that same week, the car breaks down, your son needs braces, a tree falls on the roof. It never fails. **Maybe you feel like you can't trust money.**

Whatever your story and relationship with money is, it's likely rooted in your childhood and what you learned about money from your parents. Maybe you were constantly told "Honey, we can't afford that," or you watched your parents struggle with their own dysfunctional relationship with money, and lo and behold … you can now see some similarities with your money relationship.

Or maybe you have a story like Suzy Prudden. She was born rich and grew up in a very wealthy home. Boarding school, vacations in Europe, chauffer picking her up at school ... you get the idea. And yet, her mother was constantly telling them how they were broke.

It was very confusing to be surrounded by all of that wealth, but to be constantly told they didn't have money. So, she had no clarity around money. She knew how to spend it and how to make it, but she didn't know how to manage it.

So, when she became famous and ended up on Oprah, she then followed some bad guidance around money, and ended up homeless.

As you can imagine, she lost all self-respect. How did she do that to herself? Who gets on Oprah and ends up homeless and flat broke only a few months later?

But, it makes sense if you've been fed conflicting ideas around money your entire life.

To pull herself out of her situation, she went on a spiritual journey that centered on money, changing the foundation of her relationship with it.

If your relationship with money is such that you spend your time worrying about it, complaining about it, insulting it, calling it bad or evil ... or worse, maybe you don't even like money ... why would money want to hang around with you?

As Suzy says, money is just like anything else out there; it only wants to hang out with people who like and appreciate it. People need to fall in love with money. People like to be loved; money likes to be loved. The more you love money, the more it will want to hang around you.

Did reading that just make you squirm?

Okay, so first, just because you fall in love with money or love money doesn't mean you have to put money above all else in your life and become some sort of nasty person. I suspect you have many things you love in your life - your parents, your siblings, your partner, your kids, your pets, your friends, your hobbies, maybe even your work - so why would adding money to that list do anything but simply add another beautiful dimension to your life? Wouldn't feeling supported and loved by money make you feel less stressed in your life?

Money doesn't have the power to change you. Only YOU have the power to change you.

Having money or not having money isn't going to change you, nor will loving or hating money change you.

Unless you let it change you.

Now, if the whole idea of falling in love with money makes you uncomfortable, wait until you hear what Morgana Rae, World's Leading Relationship with Money Coach, teaches.

Morgana Rae is a mentor to many of today's most successful coaches and trainers. While other coaches speak about money as energy, a tool, or a measure of value (all true), Morgana says, "I don't know how to have a relationship with energy, or a measure of value. I had to imagine money was a *person* before I could change the relationship."

When Morgana started her coaching business in 1996, she was a great student. She whizzed through all her coaching and business training classes easily, her clients loved her, and she was getting great testimonials from movie stars and Hollywood directors.

And yet, she had a deep, dark secret: she was failing miserably at getting paid. Even when people wanted to give her money, it was as if she had super powers that pushed money away. At her lowest moment, she was struggling to make $100 a month, living in one of the most expensive cities in the world.

During one particularly dark night of despair, she made a decision that money needed to be her next area of spiritual growth, and she became deeply curious about what was going on inside of her that couldn't BE with money.

In the middle of her examining her relationship with money, her coach asked her the following: "If your money were a person, who would your money be?"

Just as he asked the question, a vision popped into her head of a big, dirty, violent biker who terrified her. He felt dangerous, and she felt compelled to create distance from him. Before seeing this "Money Monster," Morgana never knew she had those feelings of fear and distrust toward money. Personhood made her unconscious relationship visible. In that moment, she realized she could never have money in her life if THAT was how she felt about her money.

Morgana decided she had enough of scary biker dude representing her money, and she got rid of him.

That process brought to light a new problem, she says, as she thought, "Oh crap - I just got rid of the only relationship with money I've ever had."

So Morgana asked herself who she could want in her life so much that she'd be willing to keep that person, even if it was money. She instantly imagined a handsome, romantic young man, dressed in a tuxedo and carrying red flowers. He wanted to woo her.

This was her "Money Honey," and she realized her Money Honey ALWAYS wanted to be there for her - he loved her and wanted to be with her.

She asked him what he needed from her, and he told her to stop treating him like a monster.

The day after she did this, she got four new coaching clients who paid her double what she had ever charged before. And the clients kept coming, paying more and more, from all over the planet. She went from $100 a month to $100,000 months, by changing her relationship with money from fear to love and generosity.

This illustrates another great point:

There's gold in your shadows and treasure in your failures, so honor that.

Morgana took her experience and created a very powerful exercise, which her clients have used to make millions of dollars, and you may want to do it as well.

The secret: making money a PERSON, because that makes the relationship real.

You start with the monster - everything you don't want - and that creates the momentum necessary for meeting the monster's opposite: the lover, the Money Honey.

Because guess what? When the bad stuff is gone, all that's left is love.

EXERCISE: Find Your Money Honey

(Morgana's signature Financial Alchemy® process)

There are six steps to this process – be sure to complete the entire exercise in one sitting:

Step One: Uncover the Root Cause behind your negative relationship with money. Anything in your life - or the world - that has ever made you feel undeserving, unloved, or unsafe (especially the stuff that doesn't appear to be money-related) is going to be very useful to note here.

Step Two: Now imagine there's a person responsible for these terrible events and experiences. This will be your Money Monster. When you create it, make it big and all bad.

Step Three: When the monster is real enough and bad enough, obliterate it by any means necessary. Leave no bloody bits.

Step Four: When your Money Monster is completely gone, imagine meeting your Money Honey - the total opposite of your monster. While the monster was all bad, your Money Honey is all love.

(Note: Money as a lover works better than other archetypes. Morgana has coached thousands of clients through this, and there's something about loving and being loved that elevates our self-worth and powers of attraction like nothing else.)

Step Five: Dialogue with your new Money Honey. This is your chance to find out what your money wants for you, and what your money needs from you to stay with you. Take advantage of this wisdom!

Step Six: Commit to a single, concrete, measurable action based on what your new Money Honey asked of you in Step Five that will let you know this relationship has changed. That's where the magic happens! For example, when Katie Curtin kept her commitment to her Money Honey, she made $10,000 a few hours later, out of the blue. When Elliot Malach met his Money Honey and took his action, he received $87,000 six hours later. Pam L. had her first $250,000 sales month when she did the exercise. (Not all results are that big and that fast, but they can be.)

Build a relationship with your Money Honey for life. When something doesn't go the way you thought it would, address your Money Honey and ask him/her why.

There may come a day where you need to "upgrade" your Money Honey and do the exercise again. That's terrific! Every time you slay a monster, you create a more powerful and intimate relationship with your Money Honey, and the financial results tend to get much bigger.

Lastly, whatever you decide to do to transform your relationship with money, know it's a *practice*. Suzy Prudden advises that it doesn't happen automatically. If you want a new relationship with money, it's going to take time and practice.

So, now that we've covered creating a new relationship around money, it's time to dig into one of the most misunderstood "laws" around attracting money.

Chapter 11
THE TRUTH ABOUT THE LAW OF ATTRACTION

In 2006, the movie "The Secret" came out.

If you haven't seen the movie, it was basically a simplified version of the Law of Attraction, which states, "What you focus on expands." So, if you're broke and you focus on being broke (such as worrying or complaining about being broke), you'll stay broke. But, if you focus on being rich, then you'll become rich.

When the movie came out, I was in the middle of my quest to attract more money into my life and build a multiple six-figure business. So, of course I decided to give it a shot. In addition, I had a lot of friends and associates who swore by LOA, so I was predisposed to believe in it.

And, it didn't take long for everything to come crashing down on me.

You see, telling someone who is a worrier to stop worrying because all they're going to do is attract more worry into their life is like telling a dog to stop drooling before you feed it. It doesn't work. And, even more than that, all it does is make things worse.

I spent about six months stuffing my worry and anxiety down, forcing myself to think "happy" thoughts about money. Except, stuffing your feelings doesn't make them go away. All it does is make you sick, and that's exactly what happened to me.

And, to add insult to injury, my business tanked during those six months. I couldn't do anything to attract income. So, every day, my anxiety and worry grew, and every day, I kept trying to squash those feelings and "think happy thoughts."

Finally one day I had enough.

It seemed like no matter how hard I tried to focus on attracting money, I was making less and less. Clearly, the Law of Attraction wasn't working - or at least it wasn't working for me. So, I threw my hands up in the air and let myself worry.

It took a bit of time, but my business bounced back and I decided the whole LOA thing was just a crock. Plus, around that same time, I was hearing rumblings from others that the movie was a crock, and that other people were having similar experiences to mine.

Years later, when I started telling this story to some of my friends and clients who were LOA experts (two to note are Eva Gregory, who you already met, and Jeanna Gabellini, Creator of Five Star Client Formula, whose story I'll share in a minute).

These were the ladies who told me the movie had oversimplified LOA.

Yes, what you focus on expands. And yes that includes your thoughts. BUT your thoughts are a very small piece of the puzzle. What is more important is your FEELINGS.

So, if you're FEELING worried, angry, sadness, etc. that's what you're going to attract. And if you're FEELING joy, gratitude, peacefulness, love, abundance, that's what you're going to attract.

In other words, by bottling up my anxiety and worry, that's pretty much all I was able to feel, and all I was attracting. It didn't matter what my thoughts were - my thoughts didn't do jack, because my feelings were so intense.

Which is why feeling your feelings and letting them move through you is so important. (Remember what I shared earlier about tapping, and the Spring Cleaning exercise.)

Once you've felt your "negative," fear-based emotions and let them pass, then you can work on shifting your emotions and thoughts to attracting more love and abundance.

(And don't forget what Morgana said earlier – it's all about finding the gold in your shadows and the treasure in failure. She too thinks all this talk about raising your vibration and always being happy is not the key to true happiness and being emotionally healthy. When we try and pretend we don't feel our darker emotions - when we believe we're too spiritually evolved or whatever - we're treating them as if they don't have value. The big problem with that is that we need to honor the dark in us if we want to get to the light. And never forget that just because we reach the light doesn't mean the dark isn't still there, and still needs to be honored.)

Jeanna Gabellini explains that if someone is struggling with thoughts and worries around the "Am I going to make enough?" question, that person is stuck in that "not having enough" energy. So, everything they do will be tainted with that "not having enough" energy.

To exemplify this concept, remember what Kendra E. Thornbury talked about earlier. If you're stuck in fear-based emotions, (for instance, you're worried about money and you bring in money when you're worried about it, but the money you bring in is laced with fear-based emotions), while yes, you can pay your bills in the short term, you may end up paying a much higher price for that money in the long term.

When you're stuck in the "not having enough" energy, it will likely also morph into a confidence problem. Not only will your ideal clients be able to feel your lack of confidence, but you won't be able to take a stand for your ideal clients when you're making a sales call, and thus, you won't be able to make the sale.

So, this ends up being a vicious cycle where the more you worry about "not having enough," the more you'll end up not being able to attract more clients and money, and so on.

What Jeanna recommends is to shift your thoughts not by focusing on money or sales, but to something else that won't have that same energy charge. In addition, doing so also helps to shift your focus on making money fun, versus it being a struggle or a burden or a hard push.

For instance, if you get a new client at your new rate, you may worry that it's a fluke. So, you start protecting yourself - after all, you may not get another one.

But, that's not what you want to do. Instead, you should move forward like you intend and expect for more money to come in. Ask yourself "What's in my wheelhouse that I can rock?"

Jeanna has firsthand knowledge about this. A few years back, she went through a year where her income dropped like a rock.

Needless to say, this is was a source of great embarrassment and shame for her. Here she was calling herself an extreme abundance coach, yet she was making no money.

For almost a year she struggled with this. Nothing worked. No matter what she tried or how much she pushed.

Finally, she surrendered.

She surrendered to not making money, and she made peace with it. She let go of the shame.

Next she changed the question she had been asking.

Instead of asking, "What can I do to make more money?" (which was causing stress and not working), she started asking, "What can I do right now?/What's in my control right now?"

And, what she realized she could do is take amazing care of the four clients she had left. Quite honestly, she had neglected them a bit in her mad rush to generate more income, but she decided it was time to turn all of that around and start treating them like major VIPs.

She then made a plan to pay down the debt she had accumulated, and she became grateful for any money that came in, even if it was only ten bucks. She decided she wasn't going to rush the process - if it took five years to turn everything around, then that's what it took. If she had to file bankruptcy, that's what she would do.

She had a free product – a CD she would send out - and every time she received a request for a free CD, she would appreciate it and think about how it was going to net her $10,000.

She surrendered.

She didn't give up. She simply surrendered to what was happening.

Nine months later, she paid off her debt and got herself back up to a six-figure business. And, the best part is she never backslid - every year since then, she's made more money.

No matter what your situation looks like right now, it IS possible to turn it around.

Below I've summarized the steps and questions to help you do so.

Exercise: Turn Your Energy Around

- 💜 Change the question you're asking yourself to "What can I do right now in my business?" Or, if you don't have a business: "What can I do right now in my life/job etc.)?" And once you get the answer, do it. (And if it is small - such as give great customer service, don't discount it. Do it.)

- 💜 Surrender to what's happening. Stop trying to fight it or push through it or force something or spin around endlessly in your head. Pause and breathe.

- 💜 Be grateful and appreciative of any and all money that shows up in your bank account, no matter how small. (This also includes celebrating any existing clients.)

- 💜 Whenever you can, make things fun! Have fun with your sales and marketing. Play games with it. Ask yourself questions such as "What's a fun game to play as I raise my rates from $350 to $1000?" Get creative.

Okay, so we're almost done with the woo-woo money-attraction strategies. In the next chapter, I cover a few more important ones, like affirmations, how to manifest money, and what to do when you feel like you're doing everything, and it's still not working.

Chapter 12
AFFIRMATIONS, MANIFESTATIONS AND WHAT TO DO WHEN YOU'RE DOING IT ALL AND IT'S STILL NOT WORKING

What this chapter is actually about is the power of the word, and how you can use that power to rewire your brain.

Let's start with affirmations.

Affirmations

Affirmations are phrases you repeat that are designed to change the way you think about something. So, for instance, if you're struggling to attract money into your life, you may say (and repeat) an affirmation like, "Money flows to me easily and effortlessly."

It's important to write affirmations in present tense and in the positive - so saying something like, "I won't be broke anymore" isn't a good affirmation. Neither your subconscious nor the Universe processes words like "won't," "can't," or "no" - so what you're actually putting out there is, "I will be broke."

Instead, say, "I am fully supported and have enough money for all my needs."

You can use affirmations for anything you're struggling with in your life - finding a relationship, losing weight, building a successful business, improving your finances. But there is a trick to it.

In fact, Suzy Prudden talks about how most people who are teaching the concept of affirmations are doing it wrong.

The typical way you're taught to create affirmations is to focus on where you want to go. So, if you want to be a millionaire, you may have an affirmation that says, "I am a millionaire."

The problem with that is if you aren't a millionaire, your mind will argue with you. And if your mind is arguing with you about your affirmation, you're not going to be able to reprogram your thoughts. (You also don't want to say, "I will become a millionaire" because then you're putting it out there that this will happen sometime in the future, versus something that's happening now.)

Basically you've skipped a step - and that step is to say, "Now it's safe for me to be a millionaire." Or, "Now I'm willing to be okay with being a millionaire."

Tell your brain it's okay to be a millionaire.

Once you've come up with your affirmations, say them *all the time*. Post them on 3x5 cards in places where you'll see them multiple times a day. Write them out and say them out loud ten times a day.

Your brain is always going to be right, which is why affirmations can be so powerful. Once you've repeated it enough, your brain starts to believe the affirmations, and then, it will start making them come true.

This is also why you want to be careful about other things you say to yourself, not just affirmations. If you find yourself saying things like, "Life is hard," or, "I'll never make any money," you'll be right.

You're *always* going to be right, so what do you want to be right about?

Now we all can make excuses about why we can't do something. But the point isn't the excuse. The point is that you're telling your brain *you can't do something* (sort of like an affirmation in reverse).

Suzy says you don't need the reason why you can't do something. Reasons are boring. If you say you can't do something, then you can't. It doesn't matter why.

Along with correctly using affirmations, Suzy also says that the real trick to getting what you want is to *look at your habits*.

One of Suzy's habits she had to change is her habit of worrying about money. What she recommends doing is to practice noticing your habit – become very aware of it.

When you see yourself worrying, tell yourself you're doing it again.

(Now, for me, this sort of advice didn't work at all to stop my worrying habit, but if it works for you, fabulous!)

Ask and You Shall Receive ... Are You Even Asking?

Cory Michelle, Motivational Speaker and Personal Life Coach, is a magical and potent facilitator for people who desire to live a life of ease, joy and magic. She has transformed her life from hard, frustrating, and struggling for money to one in which she receives everything she asks for.

Cory is proof that the "ask and you shall receive" universal principal really works ... and she's made it her mission to teach her clients exactly how to use it properly, so they too can experience the magic.

The thing is, we are generally taught to be "good and right." We avoid being "bad or wrong," and we fear failure. But that mindset leaves us perpetually seeking the "right" answer for creating life. The truth is, no one creates his or her life in the same way, and there is no magical formula that works for everyone. When someone is seeking more money or financial freedom, to have enough to support herself, or even if she longs to be "ultra" wealthy, she must look at her relationship with money, and what she is *actually* asking for.For example, if Joe can't pay his bills, he might naturally say, "I need money for my bills." Then, the only money that comes to him is just enough for those bills. If he IS able to create more than that minimal amount, he will also likely create more bills to pay, inadvertently. To reframe this into the proper way to ask and receive, Joe could say:

What would it take to have more money in my life?

What actions can I take to have plenty of money?

What would it be like to have plenty of money for everything my body and I would like to have? Can you sense the different energy there?

When you ask open-ended questions like the above, the universe and all the molecules in it can contribute to answering them.

The first step toward making the "ask and receive" principal work for you is to determine where you are, right now. Are you:

1. Not asking at all?

2. Asking in a way that is limiting what you receive?

3. Asking for everything you'd like to have as your life, and in your life, with open-ended questions?

One you determine where you are, and how to ask different questions, you're ready to practice asking the new types of questions.

Following are some of the ones Cory has used herself to create her magical life, so you can ask them too:

- What else is possible here?

- How does it get better than this?

- What is possible that I've decided I cannot ask for or have?

- What question could I ask now?

- What can I choose to create more money right away?

- What can I choose to create more ease and joy right away?

- What is crazy possible today?

- What would I truly like my life to be like?

- What would it be like to have plenty of money all the time?

Cory Michelle started with these basic questions, and she says the key to having them work in your life is to not seek the answers, but be open and curious to the awarenesses that show up. Curiosity is the greatest secret to having the "ask and receive" principal work for you. When you are being curious, you are open to possibilities. But when you are seeking what you think is the "right" answer, you can only see what you've decided is going to be right. That is a limitation. To open to the infinite possibilities available at any time, be curious and ask, what IS possible here?

Manifesting 101

Anastasia Netri had built a successful coaching practice in the transformation industry: an industry composed of entrepreneurs who are committed to changing the world and making a difference. (Sometimes they call themselves "conscious" entrepreneurs or "spiritual" entrepreneurs or "creative" entrepreneurs or "heart-centered" entrepreneurs or "messengers" or "agents of change." They have other names too, but these are the most common.)

Anastasia was a great coach. She made a lot of money coaching other entrepreneurs on how to build a successful business.

The problem was, she didn't really like being a business coach. She had wanted to be a life coach, but was told there was more money in the business side, so she switched her focus to that.

On the surface, it looked like the right choice. She was making a lot of money, she had the freedom that comes with owning her own business, and she was coaching (although she was doing business coaching, not life coaching).

But, she wasn't happy. In fact, she was the exact opposite - she was constantly anxious, which manifested in a 40-lb weight gain.

She finally realized that money didn't make her happy (which was a shock because she had basically spent years chasing money, and making it the focus of her life). Part of the reason it didn't make her happy is because she discovered she had built her business on a foundation of fear: fear of not having enough, fear of losing what she had, fear of how her peers would judge her and think of her, etc. And, as you hopefully know by now, when you build something on a foundation of fear, what you sacrifice is your happiness and peace of mind.

She ended up closing down her biz-coaching business, and is currently rebuilding her business into something sustainable that also feels calm and peaceful. And, yes, she is making money with it!

I realize this is a strange way to begin a section on manifesting money, but that's because the key to manifesting whatever you want - including money - is to *feel connected to something bigger.*

Thinking that having money will create calm in your life is an illusion. It's not true. Money magnifies what you're lacking in your life and makes it bigger.

Abundance is a flow; the requirement for experiencing abundance is letting go, surrendering, and trusting. But, in order to be able to let go and surrender and trust, you need to feel connected to safety and love and something *bigger*, which helps to keep you grounded.

You need to believe you'll always be taken care of - that God has your back, and if you just relax and trust, your needs will be met.

And yes, I get that this sounds easier than it actually is.

Stick with me.

If you've ever tried manifesting something and it hasn't worked, it's likely because of the illusion that whatever you manifest will change your being.

Let's use money as an example. You might think when you manifest money, you'll feel taken care of. (Or, when you manifest money, you'll finally feel happy, or finally relax.)

But, money can't do that for you. As I've mentioned, money can't change your BEING. So, the manifestation doesn't work.

However, if you practice something Anastasia calls "aligned manifestation," you can change all of that.

First off, you don't really need to learn how to manifest - you're already doing it.

Everything you see in your life is an accurate manifestation of what you've been manifesting, even if you've been doing it subconsciously or unconsciously.

Now, you may not like what you've manifested and want to manifest something else.

To do that, start with a clear intention.

For instance, "I would like to manifest money."

The next step is to bring the manifestation into 3-D form.

You do that by associating the manifestation with what you currently have.

So, this step might look like this: I would like to manifest money and this manifestation is a natural and organic extension of what I already have - so manifesting money is a natural and organic extension of my big heart/how much I love to coach my clients/my strong intuition/etc.

You also may want to write it down, because when you see it on paper, it's really powerful.

Whatever it is you want to manifest, it's already there inside you. All you need to do is see the actual truth to bring it into form.

What to Do When You're Doing It All and It's Still Not Working

First, this problem isn't that uncommon, and it's totally fixable.

Remember to keep doing the breathing exercises to feel into your emotions.

This section is for you if you're doing everything I've recommended in this book, and money still isn't flowing to you. In other words, you're working on releasing your blocks, doing your gratitude exercise, saying your affirmations … and nothing is working.

To begin with, you may just need to give things a little more time to work. You didn't build all of these blocks and obstacles to making money overnight. It may take a little more time to undo them before you start to reap the rewards.

Second, you might have a problem believing.

It's like Kate Beeders, Mindset, Money, and Marketing Expert says: **"It's not just saying it, it's believing it."**

Your instinct right now may be to argue that you DO believe, but the truth is, you might not … because deep down, you have fear and doubts. If you really did believe it, you would already have the results!

And then you make it all worse because you beat yourself up when it doesn't work. You compare yourself to others who you believe have the results you want for yourself, and you make yourself less worthy than them.

Kate shares a story about a real estate agent who came to her because every single deal she had was falling through. When they dug into it, it became clear that the real estate agent was saying to herself, "I'm only getting X for this deal, and that totally isn't enough. It's not worth it."

So, instead of coming from a place of gratitude for what she was getting, she was unhappy because it wasn't enough. As a result, the deal would fall apart.

Once she made a shift and felt grateful and happy about what she was getting for each deal, no matter how small, then they started going through.

The point is, it's not enough to say it.

You have to actually feel it.

So, how do you do that? If you just launched a new program, and you wanted to sell ten programs but you only sell five, how do you become grateful for the five you sold instead of angry you didn't sell the ten?

Kate says the secret is to take small steps. Shift your vibration one tiny step at a time.

First, acknowledge the anger. You're upset you didn't get ten sales - don't push that down or numb it or run away from it. Feel it. You didn't get your ten sales.

Next, look for something small you can feel grateful and happy about. You can be happy you actually DID make a sale. That's huge! Not everyone who launches a program makes a sale.

And, maybe you can be excited about the people who bought. Maybe you can be super excited to work with them.

And maybe you can be excited about the idea that it IS only five, because it's the first time you've run the program, and with only five people enrolled, you can make sure you work the bugs out and still have super-happy clients.

See how this works?

Eventually, you can shift your mindset to feeling happy and grateful for what you have, which will then raise your vibration to attract even more.

In addition, Kate shared something else to pay careful attention to, if you're having difficulty attracting money into your life.

Take a look at what words you're using.

We're all energy, right? And the words we speak are vibrations of that energy, which means we'll attract it back. (This is the Law of Magnetism: what you put out there, you attract back.)

For instance, when you say, "I'm so overwhelmed," you attract that overwhelm energy back to you. Plus, what makes it even worse is that you're saying I AM - so you're actually saying YOU ARE overwhelmed. (This also applies to saying something like, "I'm broke.")

Kate again recommends shifting your wording slightly to a different, less negatively-charged word like "challenged" instead of "overwhelmed." That way, you still acknowledge how you feel, yet the new phrase ("I'm feeling challenged") carries a slightly less negative weight. Say, "I'm feeling challenged right now." That changes the energy you're attracting back. Or you can say, "I'm choosing not to spend my money on X right now."

As a result, you'll be able to shift into positive energy faster, and attract more abundance into your life, resulting in more money, clients, and amazing opportunities!

And if you do catch yourself saying something like, "I'm overwhelmed," immediately say, "I take it back" and then say it in a different, better way.

And with that, we wrap up the woo-woo part of the attracting money strategies, and we move to the more practical tools in the next chapter.

Chapter 13
PRACTICAL MONEY-ATTRACTION TIPS

First, a little disclaimer:

When I talk about practical money-attraction strategies, I'm not talking about strategies like budgeting, or going out and getting a second job.

I would classify these strategies as the more "practical" mindset strategies around attracting money.

This chapter is for those of you who know you need to get your mindset in line with how much money you want to make, but who don't resonate with stuff like Law of Attraction and affirmations.

I'm going to start with Ali Shanti/Alexis Neely (she goes by both names), Founder of Eyes Wide Open Life and author of the upcoming book, *Enough! The Money Wake-Up Call to Reclaim Your Time, Energy and Attention in Service to a Life Worth Living.*

Ali provides a balanced view approach to the attraction of money that has both a metaphysical component and a highly-practical piece.

Ali says most people are inadvertently blocking their desires with a simple lack of clarity, and gaining that clarity – that knowing around what you actually need – is the first step in bringing in the money you desire. A lack of clarity can show up in a few different ways:

- 💜 A consistent focus on "just getting by," which results in never having enough.

- 💜 A "big life" vision that is too far off from where you are right now to be realistic, which leads you to incorrect subsequent steps.

- 💜 A perpetual "fog" of not knowing, resulting in wasted time and energy.

But once you have clarity, receiving what you need next is actually quite easy. Usually, you just have to ask for it.

Once you ask, receiving can come in many forms, such as from loans, sales, investments, investors, etc. (And often, from mysterious sources you'd never expect!)

When you stop seeing money as a compass for your life, telling you where to go, you can turn it into fuel for all of your heart's desires.

Here's how you do it:

- 💜 Stop the incessant focus on making as much money as possible, and get clear on exactly what you need next.

💜 In order to do that, you need to know where you are now in relationship to the three dimensions of desire.

💜 Once you know that, you can map out the path from where you are now to where you are going next, and clearly ask for what you need to get there.

The three dimensions of desire to consider are:

1. The minimum amount of money you need to be happy. And by minimum, Ali does mean minimum, and by happy, she does mean happy! We are not just talking about "getting by." We're talking about you being genuinely happy.

2. The minimum you need to be of service. For this one, you want to free up as much of your time as possible to focus your energy and attention on that which serves most. So perhaps having a housekeeper and a personal assistant is part of your minimum to be of service. Maybe you need to "up" your self-care to maximize your energy, so getting regular massages is part of the minimum. You get the idea.

3. What would you prefer, if you could afford it? For this one, think luxuries you don't need, but you sure would like! Maybe you prefer to fly first class. Maybe you would buy a more expensive car, or take more upscale vacations. In this category, you also include "extra" amounts you

186

want to invest, perhaps into things like your kids' college education, other people's businesses, real estate, or the stock market.

Once you are clear on those three dimensions, you will want to clarify where you are now in relationship to them.

Not yet at your minimum to be happy? Well, that's your next step! Don't even think of the other ones until you've created an income model that gets you there.

At your minimum to be happy, but not yet at your minimum to be of service? Focus on asking for (or finding) the money to free up your time by hiring more support, or by releasing a conflict that's taking more creative energy than it's worth.

At your minimum to be of service, but not yet at your preferred? Now you can decide if those little luxuries are worth sacrificing the time you'll have to invest to earn more money. Or perhaps you'll start to discover new ways to earn more money with your time, leveraging your efforts.

Already at your preferred? Maybe now's the time to breathe a sigh of relief, relax, and finally stop pushing yourself so hard! Maybe you focus on re-discovering who you are, and re-evaluate your choices, now that money isn't the main motivator it once was.

Once you see where you stand, and where you could be standing, you may need to put together a plan to get there. And that's perfectly okay. Sometimes you need to give your mind what it needs to let things go. And if your brain is only focused on making money, perhaps what you need is a plan to either change how you live and/or how much you make to fit where you want to be. Maybe you even need a "comeback plan," in case things don't go the way you want them to.

As Ali puts it, our mind needs something to focus on, so by giving that focus to our mind, it won't end up distracting us. (For example, you don't have a marketing plan, so every time your income dips in your business, you spin around wasting a lot of time trying to make money, whereas if you had a marketing plan in place, your mind would have something to focus on, which would allow YOU to stay focused and productive.)

Something else to remember is that your mind isn't the only thing that can distract you. Your environment - even your clothes - can, as well.

Back when I was a freelancer and wanted to attract new clients, one of the things I would always do is organize my files. I would clean out all the files and notes from completed clients and box them away, leaving space for new clients to come in. (Nature abhors a vacuum, and if your old clients are still taking up space in your office, how can new clients come in?)

This actually worked really well for me. So if you're someone who is surrounded by clutter and stacks of paper in your office, maybe taking some time to clean up is exactly what needs to happen to start the money flow. (This is actually surprisingly effective. Sometimes a big purge is actually what's needed to get the energy moving again.)

Kendall SummerHawk, Leader in Certified Coach Training for Women Entrepreneurs, is also big on taking a closer look at your environment. As she puts it, people surround themselves with things that represent their past. On top of that, there can be a lot of trapped emotions in clutter. (Think of how exhausting it is once you actually take the time to clean out the clutter.) If your work space is surrounded by all that clutter, how on earth can you get anything done?

You need space to work - physical space, time space, and the space of energy.

Kendall also recommends having a daydreaming space that's completely uncluttered, so you can really dream BIG. (How can you dream big if you're feeling constrained by your lack of space?)

Another thing to look at is what you're wearing when you go to work. This is especially crucial if you're a work-at-home entrepreneur.

If it's three in the afternoon, and you haven't brushed your teeth or gotten out of your pjs, how does that feel? Can you really be someone who attracts high-end clients dressed like that?

(Now, yes, some people are able to get away with wearing torn jeans and dirty, stained tee shirts and make great money, but the difference is they're doing it and succeeding right now. If you're not happy with your level of income and you do dress this way, perhaps starting your day with a shower and a clean outfit that feels good when you wear it is in order. Kendall isn't the only one who talks about this - Elizabeth Gilbert brought it up in her book *Big Magic*. If you aren't getting creative ideas, maybe get out of those disgusting sweat pants that haven't been washed in a week and fix yourself up. Perhaps a little makeup is even in order. Elizabeth says you want to make yourself appealing and attractive to creative ideas – otherwise, why would they want to hang around with you? The same can be said for money.[10]

Along with taking a look at your environment and your clothes, stay connected to how money comes in. Check your bank account regularly. Keep track of all the money coming in. You may even want to create a spreadsheet or have a place in your calendar/organizer where you write down all your deposits. The more you focus on the money coming in, the more money will end up coming in. (Bonus points if you have a plan for managing your money AND you follow it. If the Universe sees you're able to manage what it gives you, then it will be more likely to give you more.)

EXERCISE: What If?

Kendall shares the following exercise, to help you see the "what if" that could be possible for you.

10   Elizabeth Gilbert, *Big Magic* (2016)

Begin by writing down the most you've ever charged on a piece of paper.

Now, add a zero at the end of that. So, if you charged $50 an hour, it becomes $500. Or if you have a $500 coaching package, it becomes $5,000.

If you're like most people, your initial reaction is to freak out when you see that. So, start by pausing and taking a breath. Then ask yourself, as someone who charges that amount, what do you focus on during the day? What do you wear? What do you get rid of in your environment? What do you tolerate? What is the quality of your relationships?

Start to feel yourself becoming the person you want to be. And, as you do, you'll become more and more aligned with charging more.

Kendall is a big believer in the theory that the way you do money is the way you do everything.

She's created an assessment called the Sacred Money Archetypes®.

According to Kendall, there are eight different archetypes, and when you learn which one you are, a lot of things start to fall into place. It's also a great way to learn your strengths, and shadow side around money, so you can maximize the good and minimize the shadow side. You can learn more about this assessment in the Resources section.

Above all, remember to be gentle with yourself throughout this process. It's not easy to shift your relationship with money so you start attracting more of it. And it's not going to happen overnight. But, regardless, I'm really proud of you for coming this far and taking responsibility for your money situation. You rock!

The next section is for entrepreneurs and would-be entrepreneurs, as it's focused on marketing and growing your business in a love-based way. (If you need a refresher on the love versus fear-based theory, see the Introduction, but in a quick nutshell, what I'm talking about is building and marketing your business on a foundation of love-based emotions, rather than fear-based emotions. Remember, all emotions fall under either love or fear, so it's really up to you which way you want to go when it comes to how you build and market your business.)

The following tips aren't in my other love-based business books, so be sure to keep reading even if you've read the others. (And if you want more step-by-step advice and exercises to help you build a love-based business, you'll definitely want to check out my other books.)

If you have no interest in business, you may want to skip the next section and read the final chapter, where I pull it all together and talk about how you can go forward with your Money and Mindset Breakthrough Plan.

Part 4

LOVE-BASED BUSINESS AND MARKETING STRATEGIES

Chapter 14
MARKET AND GROW YOUR BUSINESS IN A LOVE-BASED WAY

Before I dive into specific marketing strategies, I thought I'd start with a great map that comes from Emerald Peaceful GreenForest (in the past she has also gone by the name Amethyst Wyldfyre), the Empress of Empowerment, from The Empowered Messenger. It's called The Map of Messenger Mountain.

It's designed to give you a conscious way to choose your next step when it comes to growing your business. You can use it to identify where you are now, and what the perfect next step for you to keep growing your business might be.

The Map of Messenger Mountain (aka Stages of Business Growth)

There are seven steps on the map. As we go through each, envision yourself moving up the side of a mountain.

The acronym for the seven steps is AWESOME.

Now, one thing to note before we dig into the steps: it's very possible you may hop around the different steps, or get stuck in one. You also might find yourself going back and forth between a couple (for example, moving between S and O is very common).

You might also get to the top, collapse, and fall halfway back down the mountain.

This is not a straight, linear path, and the way in which everyone follows the map is going to look a little different. But, the beauty of having a map is you'll have some idea of where you are now, and what you need to do to move on to the next step.

Step One - A for Awakening. Until you're awake, you don't even know what the mountain is, or that it exists.

Often, your awakening occurs because you hear or learn from someone else who is awake - maybe it's a Facebook post, a speaker you hear, a book you read (maybe even this book!), or maybe it happens in conjunction with a life event.

For Emerald, her awakening happened when she hurt her knee skiing. Suddenly, she became aware of a yoga class offered in the same place as where she worked out. (Keep in mind that the intent of a yoga practice is to unify the mind, body and spirit.)

It was in her yoga practice that something shifted in her. She immediately knew something changed, and she was suddenly different. She realized she could no longer continue in her very successful real estate career, because what she was really called to do was to start an energy healing business.

Step Two - W for Wandering. Once you've awoken, you'll begin wondering what just happened, and you'll wander. You may meet people who start validating your experience with their own stories. When you're wondering and wandering, you're still enmeshed in old beliefs, and you're trying to figure out how to untangle yourself from them. You also may wonder where you can find support for the new beliefs.

Step Three - E for Educate. Here, you begin educating yourself in new ways, principles and beliefs. Along with educating yourself, you also start surrounding yourself with people who are on the same path with you. You may find yourself drawn to certification programs, weekend workshops, and/or personal development retreats. Occasionally, you may experience an awakening or opening through a particular practice (like yoga), or from working with a therapist, body worker, or other alternative healer or practitioner, and the experience is so life- changing for you, you feel compelled to either tell others about it, or become educated to serve in that capacity yourself.

Step Four - S for Skills/Setting Your Business Up. At this point, you're standing at a bridge. Once you cross it, you are officially on the business path. You may need to get additional certifications or licensure to move forward with a business. You may need to start educating yourself on what it takes to run a business. You may also be setting yourself up to succeed in a business structure. The call to have a business is really strong here. It's also the point where any money issues you have start to bubble up. It makes sense, then, that this is also the place where a lot of entrepreneurs get stuck: you may be stuck getting certification after certification, or maybe you're stuck getting ready to get ready to have a business.

If you don't work on your blocks and issues around money and self-worth, you may never leave this stage.

As you work on your money and mindset issues, you may realize you need other skills than what you've developed. Maybe you need to learn how to sell or write copy or market yourself better. If you don't learn those skills, you'll also stay stuck in this S stage. In addition, you may also need to acknowledge your own self-worth, recognize the value of what you have to offer to the market, and make the fundamentals of continuously improving your relationship with money a higher priority before you can leave this stage and move on to the next.

Step Five - O for Opening for Opportunities. This is where you start opening yourself up to opportunities that allow you to become visible and get your message out there. O is where you may start to find yourself invited to speak on stages or be interviewed. However, if you haven't mastered the skills in S and/ or you're not clear about your message, you may find that O actually represents "over-giving," and you end up just "gushing" on stage - never really selling anything. Far too often, messengers are so FULL of their message and so eager to serve and inspire and activate their audience that they simply "forget" about the asking for money part. Or, they go way over the time allotted for their presentation and leave no room for making a proper and compelling offer to the audience to invest and go further with them.

Step Six - M for Monetize. This is where you finally start monetizing your message. In M, you're clear about your message and you're starting to generate consistent revenue. However, advanced money issues (or deeper money issues) may start to come up.

At M, it's clear you're running an actual business. It's not a hobby, and it's not a personal calling; it's a business.

Where you may get hung up here is if you don't really love what you created, or you fall out of love with what you created. Maybe you've put yourself in a cookie- cutter system your coaches have told you to follow, but it's not a fit for you and you struggle to make money. It may even feel difficult to make money, even though you think you should or it seems like you should. (This may be how the more advanced money issues show up.) Learning to have a clear and clean selling conversation is essential, along with being really, *really* clear on your own value and the value of what you have to offer. Of course, a business runs on money, and you must do the math so that you have certainty around exactly what you need to generate in order to not only survive, but to really, truly thrive.

Step Seven - E for Exponential Exposure. At this point, you're at the top of your game, and you start looking around at other people who have risen to the tops of their mountains to see if they would be interested in strategic alliances.

To be here, you need to be wired for wealth. Successful businesses require money to run them, every day, at all times. Consistent cash flow is key to your success and your sanity! At E, you may also be more of a "steward" of money: you're in a position to manage and grow the money that comes in to your business for the long term health of the organization and the legacy you are leaving.

Roadblocks can show up here as well. If you haven't mastered being wired for wealth, you may still find yourself challenged here until you do. You also start to realize that it's no longer about you, because you're a part of something bigger.

Once you've reached E, one of three things can happen:

1. You get entrenched in your leadership role (which can also mean you've gotten in the way of someone else stepping into their leadership role). As a leader, one of your main roles is to steward the next leaders who are coming after you, so the point may not be for you to reach the top and stay there. (You may want to ask yourself periodically if you're standing in the way of someone else stepping into a leader's role.)

2. You collapse and end up halfway down the mountain again. Or you may burst and collapse all the way to the bottom, where you will discover that you are invited to AWAKEN again into another view of your life, your business, and what may very well be your

next calling. The beauty here is that you are now skilled and have experience and knowledge that you didn't have on your first attempt to hit the peak. People often "re-brand" at this stage: sometimes up-leveling, sometimes taking on a different aspect of the original work they were doing, or sometimes simplifying or specializing even more within their existing niche.

3. You leave the industry altogether. You jump fields, but you take all of your skill, energy and power with you.

Occasionally, you will simply rise up to your personal peak and stay there, growing and expanding your body of work and creating and living your legacy, welcoming wealth in exchange for your wisdom. In this case, you're often supported and surrounded by a core tribe of diehard fans who will happily invest in just about anything you have to offer, because you've built such a solid, deep, and wide base. This happens when you are truly "wired for wealth." You become an ICON in your industry, and your work ultimately lives on after you have passed from this plane of existence.

One way to tell if you've gotten stuck or lost somewhere along the path is to look at your finances. Money is a reflection of deeper issues that are happening in your business. If you've been successful and money starts to dry up, that's a sign something is out of alignment. You may need to go back to the beginning and see what you're supposed to be doing.

If money gets tight, Emerald also recommends dropping everything and connecting with Source. You may want to ask: "Is what I'm doing still serving me? Is it serving Source/Life? Or am I being called to a different mountain, or to make a quantum leap?"

Marketing Your Business Using Your Core Wound

In Chapter Two, I introduced you to Jeffrey and his work around the core wound, to help you choose the right personal development tools for you.

Well, you can also use your core wound to help you find the perfect people you were meant to serve in your business.

In your business, you've likely created a solution that solves your core wound, so for people who share your core wound, they'll have a much bigger transformation with your solution than people who don't.

In other words, your wound hardwired you to work with this specific group of people - you're tailor-made for those people.

So, if you position your services to speak to people who share your core wound, you'll attract more of your tribe, and you'll essentially repel those who don't have your core wound.

The way this works is everyone has three problems - a "known" problem, a "secret" problem, and an "unknown" problem. The known problem is the visible problem that your tribe is talking about and actively looking for help around. The secret problem is how your tribe feels about their known problem. The unknown problem is the core wound your tribe shares in common with you, which is the root cause of the known and secret problems.

So to be truly successful, you package your services to address the known problem, you speak in marketing to the secret problem, and you deliver the transformation to shift the unknown problem related to the core wound with your products and services.

To see how this works with an actual business, let me share with you how Cory Michelle has designed her business around her core wound.

Her core wound is that she never felt like she belonged. Even before birth. She felt unwanted, like she wasn't supposed to be here.

When you feel like you don't belong, you either go into sheer rebellion, or you try and fit in.

And when you feel like you don't belong, you create an energetic barrier. Your internal conversations are about how you feel like you don't belong. You create lack, because you don't feel like you can reach out to people.

Cory Michelle thinks of it like a fog - you're creating an energetic fog so your ideal clients can't even see you, much less find you and hire you. If this is you, nothing external (like changing your marketing/pricing/messaging) will work.

What you end up doing is proving the "wrongness" – you'll say you keep trying all of this and it's still not working. You've then essentially created a whole bunch of evidence to prove that it's not working.

EXERCISE: Breaking Out of the Fog

Now, if this is you and you want to break out of that pattern, ask yourself these questions:

- ❤ Do you fit in? Do you belong?

- ❤ If you don't feel like you belong, how old were you when you figured it out?

- ❤ Who have you become that's not you, based on this belief of not fitting in?

- ❤ Would you be willing to consider you didn't come here to belong? Did you actually come here to fit in? Or did you come to create a new reality or a new world?

- ❤ What if you didn't come here to fit in - then what gift could you be to the world?

- ❤ What else is possible if you didn't fit in?

Cory Michelle felt like she was living two different lives - she felt so different than everyone else. Once she accepted that maybe she wasn't put here to fit in, it was like a fog lifted, and her clients were able to find her.

It's difficult to make invitations to your ideal prospects when you're doubting yourself, or proving yourself wrong.

Speaking of making invitations, as an entrepreneur, especially if you have an online business or use the Internet to market yourself, you're likely going to invite people to work with you via written invitation. In fact, you'll probably need a lot of things written (websites, blog posts, emails, etc.).

Keep reading for tips on how to make your writing love-based.

Love-Based Copywriting Tips

While I would definitely encourage you to check out my first two Love-Based Copy books so you can really master writing copy, below are a few more tips courtesy of Kendall and Pamelah. (And if you want to get started writing right away, you can download my complimentary Love-Based Copywriting Template. While it is most effective to use the template in conjunction with my Love-Based Copywriting Method book, if you feel like you have a good handle on love-based copy already, grab the template and get writing. See the Resources section for more information.)

Kendall SummerHawk talks about how when we write, it's not just about the words you choose to use, it's also about the energy you're feeling at the time of writing.

That's why it's so important to be in a great state of mind when you write. Kendall also encourages you to fall in love with your perfect clients. Love their challenges, love their gifts, and love what they want to achieve.

You may even want to create an ideal client vision board, or post an avatar of your ideal client, so you can connect with him or her as you write.

Another exercise Kendall recommends is to literally step into your ideal clients' shoes before you write the copy.

Kendall will stand up and take a big step forward into the metaphorical shoes of her perfect client. Then she asks him/her a series of questions like "What are your challenges? What matters to you? What keeps you up at night? What would help you most right now?"

The idea is to ask as many questions as you can think of. Get really curious.

When Kendall finishes this exercise, she thanks her ideal client, and takes a step backward, so she's back in her own shoes and starts writing.

Pamelah Landers won't write any copy unless she is really excited and clear about what she's offering. She'll wait until she's in that space before she writes any email invitations - otherwise the copy just falls flat.

Pamelah found if she's still struggling to understand what she's offering, then everyone else will be confused too, and they won't resonate with her words. The more aligned and happy she is with her offer, the better.

She's also taken a lot of pressure off herself around marketing. It used to be she would write her newsletter every Sunday night, whether she felt inspired to write or not. The problem was if she wasn't inspired to write, it would come out flat and not be a vibrational match. So, now she waits to see if she feels inspired and compelled to share. If she does, then she writes her newsletter. If not, she doesn't. (Sunday or not!)

She also thinks it's important to step away and detach. If you're struggling with your marketing, then walk away. It never works to try and force it.

Lastly, Pamelah recommends simplifying your language so people can feel the energy. People need to feel the vibration in the marketing copy you're sending them.

Your Most Important Asset as an Entrepreneur

The final point I want to leave you with also comes from Kendall, who says the biggest thing an entrepreneur needs to do is nurture and protect your self-confidence.

It takes a lot of courage to be an entrepreneur. Never forget that.

If you're feeling trapped around your struggles with money, it can greatly diminish your self-confidence.

In those moments, it's important to remember it IS just a moment. Which means it will pass. And in that moment, you have a choice - you can choose to sink into the hole and allow your self-confidence to take a hit, or you can pause and breathe.

Instead of allowing your self-talk to control you, you really can change or stop it. (See Chapter Six for tips on that Inner Mean Girl or Dude.) In those moments, you may even want to complete the following exercise.

EXERCISE: The Amazing Me

Brainstorm 30 things that are amazing about yourself. Yes, you may feel like you need to really stretch yourself, but that's the point.

Be generous with yourself. Love yourself.

You got this. xxoo

Chapter 15
CREATE YOUR MONEY-ATTRACTION PLAN

As a quick reminder, if you haven't downloaded the Money and Mindset Blueprint, you can do so right here:

http://www.LoveBasedMoney.com/blueprint

It will guide you in creating your Money-Attraction Plan in the way that works best for you.

I thought I'd share a few final tips to maximize your success with your Plan.

- Come up with a regular daily practice, which will help ground you and manage your emotions to keep you present and peaceful. (See Part Two, Chapter Four.)

- Along with your daily practice, come up with at least one daily money-attraction exercise from Part Three.

- When you hit any roadblocks around money, don't despair (or panic). Pause and breathe. All it is is a sign you need to do something. Maybe you need to do a different money-attraction exercise. Maybe it's time for some deeper work around your money issues. If you have a business, maybe it's a sign you need to do something different in your business.

- ❤ Have fun with these exercises and this book. Maybe you play games - open the book at random and do whatever exercise you find on the page you open. Maybe you try something new every day for a month. Maybe you set up a fun contest or game around one or more of the exercises. Enjoy yourself. Have a blast!

And the last thing I want to share is this: If all of this seems difficult to you, it may be helpful to keep in mind what Suzy Prudden says: "You don't grow when things are easy, and we're here to grow and evolve. Sometimes things are easy and sometimes things are hard."

Besides, your struggles with money may be the door that opens up an entire world of happiness, peace and love you don't even know exist right now. So rather than resenting taking action to change your relationship with money, maybe try being grateful for it, and open up to what it's here to teach you.

Resources

Additional books in my Love-Based Business Series, available here:

http://LoveBasedCopyBooks.com

Love–Based Copywriting Method: The Philosophy Behind Writing Copy That Attracts, Inspires and Invites (2nd Edition) (Volume 1 in the Love–Based Business Series)

This book is a great place to learn more about the philosophy behind love-based copy and love-based selling. While it does include many exercises, it's more focused on the love-based philosophy and building a solid love-based foundation. If you're look looking for a "how-to write love-based copy" book, definitely check out the next one in the series.

Companion Resource:

The Love-Based Copywriting Template:

http://www.lovebasedcopywritingbook.com/template

Love-Based Copywriting System: A Step-by-Step Process to Master Writing Copy That Attracts, Inspires and Invites (Volume 2 in the Love-Based Business Series)

This is a copywriting course in book format. This "how to" book walks you through exactly how to write love-based copy. It includes exercises, copy templates and more. If you're planning on doing any sort of writing for your business - for instance, writing emails or website copy - this book is a must-have.

Love-Based Online Marketing: Campaigns to Grow a Business You Love AND That Loves You Back (Volume 3 in the Love-Based Business Series)

All successful, profitable businesses need a marketing plan, and this book walks you through how to create a specific online marketing plan perfect for you. You'll also learn the basics about how to sell products and services online without feeling sales-y, and what might be standing in your way of successfully marketing your business.

How to Start a Business You Love AND That Loves You Back: Get Clear on Your Purpose & Passion - Build a Successful, Profitable Business

Part of the Love-Based Business Series

This book includes exercises and questions to ask yourself to make sure the heart of your business reflects what you really want it to. It's about answering the deeper questions around your business, like why you want it in the first place - because the more clear you are in your answers to those questions, the more satisfied you'll most likely be with what you eventually build.

I wrote this book for you if you don't have a business yet, but you want to get started, and you're intrigued by the idea of having a business you love and that loves you back.

Meditations with Audio:

Here are a few of my favorites - perform a quick Google search to find them:

Dr. Jeffrey Thompson's "Brainwave Meditations."

Dr. Wayne Dyer's "Moses Code."

Patt Lind-Kyle's "Heal Your Mind, Rewire Your Brain." (This is a great one for beginners.)

The Love-Based Money and Mindset Podcast Series:

All of the expert interviews I hosted can be found here:

http://www.LoveBasedBizBlog.com

Featured Experts:

Ali Shanti/Alexis Neely - Founder of Eyes Wide Open Life

http://www.eyeswideopenlife.com

Free Gift:

Money Map to Freedom

Discover what you really need and how to ask for it, so you can get into right relationship with time, money and how you get paid by creating your own Money Map to Freedom.

http://www.LoveBasedMoney.com/ali

Amy Ahlers - Coach, Speaker, Bestselling Author, Creator of Mama Truth Circle and Host of the Mama Truth Show

www.amyahlers.com

Free Gift:

Sacred Self-Care for Moms: 7 Steps to Nurturing Yourself So You Can Be the Mom You Were Born to Be

Discover a step-by-step process for creating your own, unique self-care system especially for soulful, badass moms. Taking care of yourself is sacred, not selfish, and this short powerful book will teach you how to create a sustainable, easy, joyful self-care system.

http://www.LoveBasedMoney.com/amy

Anastasia Netri - Transformational Coach for Awakening Women

http://www.anastasianetri.com/

Free Gift:

The Aligned Intention Setting Method

These nine steps will support you in feeling more aligned with what you want to create, and in bringing your desires into manifestation, while staying rooted in love and expressing your true talents and gifts.

http://www.LoveBasedMoney.com/anastasia

Christine Arylo - Spiritual Catalyst, Feminine Leadership Advisor, and Best Selling Author

http://www.ChristineArylo.com

Free Gift:

The Inner Critic Quiz

This Inner Critic Quiz will help you identify which of the 13 kinds of Inner Mean Girls you have that are sabotaging your business, bank account ad personal happiness and health - Comparison Queen? Achievement Junkie? Invincible SuperWoman? Find out, by taking the quiz!

http://www.LoveBasedMoney.com/christine

Cory Michelle Johnson - Motivational Speaker and Personal Life Coach

http://www.LoveBasedMoney.com/corymichelle

Elizabeth Purvis - Creatrix, Feminine Magic® and Founder, Goddess Business School®

http://www.ElizabethPurvis.com

Free Gift:

The Only 4 Manifesting Tools You'll Ever Need (To Call In Everything You'll Ever Desire)

Everything you need to create exactly what you want in your life and business is already here … IF you are using the right tools. Using these tools, you can create anything you truly Desire, from your heart. Without them, you leave your manifesting to chance. Discover them here:

http://www.LoveBasedMoney.com/elizabeth

Emerald Peaceful GreenForest – The Empowered Messenger – Empress of Empowerment

http://www.theempoweredmessenger.com

Free Gift:

Magical Mantras for Making More Money

What you focus your mind and your attention on expands - so if you have been thinking or worrying or wondering about the amount of money you are making, then you are actively engaged in creating a set of beliefs and experiences that will mirror back to you exactly what you are focusing on! PREPARE YOURSELF with the RIGHT TOOLS to help you to immediately eradicate the "Negative Nelly" that likes to invade your thinking with her worrisome doubts! Magical Mantras for Making More Money will help you to FOCUS on CREATING exactly what you want, and will support you to take the inspired actions that will make you and your business more profitable, while making your dreams of serving your purpose and answering your calling really real.

http://www.LoveBasedMoney.com/emerald

Eva Gregory – Founder of Leading Edge Coaching & Training, LLC.

 http://www.EvaGregory.com

Free Gift:

The Mindset Mastery Formula

Are you a Spiritual Entrepreneur longing to take your business to the next level? Download your Mindset Mastery Formula to attract a flood of clients.Hint: Over 90% of your success depends on this!

http://www.LoveBasedMoney.com/eva

Jeanna Gabellini - Creator of Five Star Client Formula

http://masterpeacecoaching.com

Free Gift:

Map to Profits

Jeanna's Map to Profits is a visual map that illustrates how she tripled her income in less than a year with ease and FUN! You'll get your own visual map to fill in with your most important "HELL YESES" for the year. If it's not a HELL YES, it doesn't go on your map!

http://www.LoveBasedMoney.com/jeanna

Jeffrey Van Dyk - Creator of the Tribal Marketing Training

http://www.jeffreyvandyk.com

Free Gift:

The 7 Unwritten Rules for Global Change Agents

In this free 7-part video series, Jeffrey Van Dyk shows you the keys to owning your authority and being a known expert in your field, so you can lead your purpose-driven mission.

If you know there's big work for you to do in the world, it's time you learn how to cut through the noise of the market and reach your people. When you do, you'll have the kind of impact you know you're meant to have and step into the world as a steward of your life's work.

http://www.LoveBasedMoney.com/jeffrey

Kate Beeders - Mindset, Money, and Marketing Expert

http://www.katebeeders.com

Free Gift:

Charge What You're Worth Checklist

Most people become entrepreneurs because they're really excited and passionate about something. The problem arises when their income level doesn't match their level of expertise. Grab your free "Charge What You're Worth" checklist now, so you can learn how to accelerate your income by owning your value and showing up in your brilliance.

http://www.LoveBasedMoney.com/kate

Kendall SummerHawk - Leader in Certified Coach Training for Women Entrepreneurs

http://www.KendallSummerHawk.com

Free Gift: Discover Your Sacred Money Archetypes®

Discover what makes YOU tick with money - in business, life & relationships – with this FREE Sacred Money Archetypes® assessment:

http://www.LoveBasedMoney.com/kendall

Kendra E. Thornbury – Spiritual Entrepreneur and Wealth Coach

http://www.kendraethornbury.com

Free Gift:

"3 Keys to Making Money Being You"

Discover how you can authentically help more people and create more money in a shorter amount of time, so you finally live your soul's purpose, while enjoying your freedom and true wealth.

http://www.LoveBasedMoney.com/kendra

Melinda Cohan – Transformation Leader and Founder of The Coaches Console

http://www.coachesconsole.com

Free Gift:

Network Your Way to an Abundant Business ... Even if You Hate Networking

In this four-part training series, you will learn how to eliminate the fears of networking, bust through the myths that hold you back, identify the three secrets to a clear and confident elevator pitch (but first we'll ditch the pitch!), and how to make networking fun and simple.

http://www.LoveBasedMoney.com/melinda

Mellissa Seaman - Intuitive Business Strategist

www.MellissaSeaman.com

Free Gift:

Soul Gift Quiz

Take the Soul Gift Quiz to learn what your Soul Gift is in just eight fun questions. You will then receive information that will help you understand how you're special at the deepest level, what your strengths and common challenges are, and how you are best suited to make money.

http://www.LoveBasedMoney.com/mellissa

Morgana Rae - World's Leading Relationship with Money Coach

http://www.MorganaRae.com

Free Gift:

4-Part Money Magnetic Video Series

When you imagine your money as a real, flesh and blood person, worthy of your deepest admiration, you embark on an amazing, love-at-first-sight affair of the heart. People who have done so have reported receiving unexpected money – tens of thousands of dollars or more! Unlock the Flow of Wealth into your Life.

http://www.LoveBasedMoney.com/morgana

Pamela Bruner - Business Coach, Author, and EFT Tapping Expert

http://www.MakeYourSuccessReal.com

Free Gift:

Tapping to Double Your Income Video Series

This free video series takes you through a tapping experience to remove your blocks around charging what you're worth. You'll immediately be able to give yourself a raise – and stay in integrity!

http://www.LoveBasedMoney.com/pamela

Pamelah Landers - Expert Relationship Wisdom for Your Work and Personal Life and Master Hand Analyst

http://www.PamelahLanders.com

Free Gift:

What the Four Heart Lines Tell You About Your Relationships

The heart lines in your hands tell you very tangibly and specifically:

1. How you express love.

2. How you want love expressed to you.

3. How you communicate your feelings.

These things are very specific to you, and it may be completely different for your partners, children, co-workers, friends, managers and lovers. Understanding them can help you understand what matters to you and what matters to others who are important to you, so you can improve your communication and trust.

http://www.LoveBasedMoney.com/pamelah

Suzy Prudden - Internationally Acclaimed Speaker, Workshop and Seminar Leader, and New York Times Best Selling Author (from before the internet)

Free Gift:

Four Proven Write Your Book Guided Visualizations AND my Creating Wealth Four Pack for Creating Wealth Consciousness (USE PASSWORD: Love-Based)

My Four Proven Write Your Book Guided Visualizations:

"Writing Your Book," "Successful Book Sales," "Build your Book into a 7-figure Business," and "Stress Free Writing"

Creating Wealth 4-Pack – mp3 Hypnosis Downloads:

"Financial Success," "Auto Suggestion - The Medium for Creating Wealth," "Creating Wealth Through Dreams," and "Faith and Belief in Creating Your Wealth"

http://www.LoveBasedMoney.com/suzy

About the Author
ABOUT MICHELE PW

Considered one of the hottest direct response copywriters and marketing consultants in the industry today, Michele PW (Michele Pariza Wacek) has a reputation for crafting copy and creating online and offline marketing campaigns that get results.

Michele started writing professionally in 1992, working at agencies and on staff as a marketing/communication/writing specialist. In 1998, she started her business as a freelance copywriter.

But she quickly realized her vision was bigger than serving her clients as a one-woman-shop. In 2004, she began the transformation to building a copywriting company.

Two years later, her vision turned into reality. The Love-Based Copywriting and Marketing Company is the premiere direct response copywriting and marketing company today, catering to entrepreneurs and small business owners internationally, including the "Who's Who" of Internet Marketing.

In addition, Michele is also a national speaker and author and has completed two novels. She holds a double major in English and Communications from the University of Wisconsin-Madison. Currently she lives in the mountains of Prescott, Arizona with her husband Paul and her 2 dogs — border collie Nick and southern squirrel hunter Cassie.

Made in the USA
San Bernardino, CA
14 February 2017